I'd Rather Read

I'd Rather Read

Your **Favourite Authors** on Their **Favourite Books**

RED TURTLE
RUPA

Published in Red Turtle by
Rupa Publications India Pvt. Ltd 2016
7/16, Ansari Road, Daryaganj
New Delhi 110002

Sales Centres:
Allahabad Bengaluru Chennai
Hyderabad Jaipur Kathmandu
Kolkata Mumbai

ISBN: 978-81-291-4206-1

First impression 2016

10 9 8 7 6 5 4 3 2 1

Contents

Introduction
Sleeping With Books

A little girl, just about four years old, is standing at the bottom of a flight of stairs. She is thin, her straight hair is cut short in a 'boy cut' and her eyes are bright yet dreamy. She clatters up the wooden staircase. There is only one room at the top. It is a study she shares with her elder sister. The little girl doesn't go to school yet, but she likes this room that is sunny with big windows that look out into the street. It contains two study tables piled with papers from her father's work and her sister's schoolbooks. Being here makes her feel big and important, like the sister she adores, who bustles off to school every morning. The little girl still goes to the neighbourhood playschool.

She enters the room and her eyes fall on the large steel trunk that lies at one end of the room. Where did it come from? She doesn't know and hasn't given it a moment's thought till now. It's painted green in colour and is huge in size. To her, it seems as though it can fit in about ten little girls like her. She bends down, lifts the latch and pulls up the top. She squats on the floor now and gazes at the treasures that lie within…

The trunk is filled with books. Books in English and Bengali. Brightly coloured shiny new ones. Dull and yellowing old ones. There are big bold drawings on the covers of some. Curly-whirly letters on some others. She already recognizes the distinctive signature of Enid Blyton on the covers of so many. There are some others from which her sister has read out bits to her. Like *Abol Tabol* that contains hilarious, nonsensical poems. On its cover there is a picture of a funny-looking man holding a horn to his ear. She picks it out and turns the pages, looking at the pictures. She smiles to herself, looking at the strange animals that have gone all topsy-turvy—the duck with porcupine quills, the giraffe with cockroach legs. Her favourite poem is called 'Gonph Churi' (The Stolen Moustache). She makes sure someone reads out this poem to her each time the book is opened. It's about a man who suddenly starts yelling that his moustache has been stolen. How is that possible? Can moustaches be stolen? The man believes so and gets into a wild temper when he is told that his moustache is very much where it always was. The picture alongside is of an irate man sitting on a chair and shouting.

She giggles, puts aside this book and pulls out another one. This one is in English, large in size with colourful pictures. It was presented recently by an uncle. It's brand new and the pages are still shiny and untouched. The spine creaks in a satisfying way as she opens the book. It is still not used to being open and shut regularly. The pages seem to be telling the story of a girl who falls down a hole in the garden, and then there are pages filled with the pictures of the many obviously funny adventures that the girl is having. She's been told that the name of the book is *Alice in Wonderland* and she can't wait to be able to read it on her own. For now, she settles down to turn the pages, sitting on the floor, next to the trunk full of books.

After a while she leans against the trunk, engrossed in the book. But something seems to be calling out to her from within that large steel cavern. It's the books. They are beckoning her to come closer. They seem to be whispering enticing words. She looks around the room and finds her soft cotton blanket, a *kantha* made by her grandmother, lying where she had left it the day before. She gathers it up in her arms. She moves a few books around in the trunk so that a cosy space opens up in the middle. She spreads the blanket there...and climbs in.

Now she is curled up with a book among the books. She can feel them poking her back through the blanket. She lets out a happy sigh and settles in. The smell of old and new books is all around her. She touches the pages and knows that she will forever love the feel of paper under her fingers. She traces the words with her eyes. She devours the pictures, trying to glean the story from them. Lying there, happy and carefree, her eyes begin to shut...

An hour later, her mother comes looking for her. She finds her daughter curled up inside the trunk, an open book across her chest, fast asleep.

That's my first memory of books. I don't know when I started loving them. Was it there in that trunk, where I made my first discoveries and loved them so much that I had to sit among them? But then, you never know why you love your parents or your siblings, do you? You love them because they are them. They have always been there for you and with you. For me, it's the same with books. We are travel companions, sleep companions, friends, adversaries. Sometimes they annoy me with their refusal to open up their secrets to me. Sometimes we stay up nights together because I need to read 'just one page more' and it ends up that I don't stop till I reach the last page. I laugh loudly in cafes while reading them. I stare at the sky, thinking about the words and ideas I have read in them. I still can't walk by a bookshelf, bookstore or library without examining the titles displayed there.

And most nights, I still fall asleep with one lying close by my side.

In this collection, we have the stories of some famous authors on how they started reading, and what they have loved reading the most. Some found their favourite books in school libraries, others found them in old forgotten bookshelves. Some went away to misty hill stations and discovered ghost stories and adventure stories there. Others retreated under the bed to take refuge from pesky cousins and read there in peace with a kindly grandmother standing guard.

Reading books is, strangely, a solitary activity—something that happens only between you and the book—and at the same time a wonderfully social one. Do you not feel a thrill of joy when you discover that a friend is reading the same book as you are? Have you had arguments about Harry Potter versus Percy Jackson, nearly coming to blows over which is better? Have you called your friends over and celebrated a dear author or character's birthday like he/she was someone real? (Psst, I know of a girl who celebrated Percy's birthday with all-blue food!)

With this book, you will be able to have these same conversations with those who not only read and love books the way you do, but also write them and have spent their lives among the written word. They know how words can twist and turn in your hands and become stories and poems and adventures and fantasies. Come, let's all jump into this magic hole and together discover the joys of reading. In this world there are no elders and youngsters, there are just stories and ways of finding the stories we love the best through reading.

Sudeshna Shome Ghosh

The Wonderful World of Books

A.P.J. Abdul Kalam

I don't remember the first book I ever read. It is almost as if books were always there in my life, a solid, tactile presence that exuded comfort and assurance. When I was growing up, I lived in a small town in southern India—Rameswaram. At the time, there were very few books available for children to read. Adults, too, mostly only read the newspapers. However, there was one person in that small town who had many books and who made sure anyone who wanted to read could do so. His name was S.T.R. Manickam and he was a freedom fighter. After dinner, I was allowed to go to his home library and look through his many books. His house was on a main road, and I felt a thrill each time I entered it.

What book would I get to read today? Manickam himself helped me choose books that I could read. They were fairy tales and biographies and books that explained everyday occurrences in simple language. Sitting there, among the tall bookshelves, the light coming feebly from some lamps, I would look at the flickering shadows of the cupboards on the walls, see my own wavering shadow among them, and then lose myself in a world of words and knowledge and imagination. That little library was my first introduction to the wonderful world of books.

Another person who showed me that it was possible to love books was my friend, brother-in-law and first mentor, Jallaluddin. He himself had studied up to the intermediate level and then had to give up studying as he needed to start working and earning. But he had an expansive, curious mind. His interests lay beyond the concerns of the island we lived on. On some evenings, he read reports from the newspapers and told me of a world beyond the one we inhabited. It was he who told me about the current political situation, news of the [Second World] War, prices of precious metals, and all other such information. I spent a lot of time with him, watching him read or writing letters for the people of the town, which they dictated to him. Somewhere, the power of the written word imprinted on my mind. I understood that to know and love reading meant the freedom to travel to any kind of world I wanted to. It could be the world of religion or philosophy—what I learnt in my Koran class. Or it could be poetry and imagination. Or it could be understanding the words of famous people and their lives.

Once I was older, I started reading more voraciously. After I finished school, I went to study physics at St Xavier's College in Tiruchirapalli. Here, I was introduced to the works of many new authors by my English teacher Rev. Father R.N. Sequeira. I started visiting the library often and my teacher, noticing this interest, would give me lists of books and authors whose works I could look for over there. For the first time, I started reading authors like Thomas Hardy, Leo Tolstoy and Walter Scott.

Have you ever stood before a shelf of books that stretches from the floor to the ceiling, looking at the names on the spines of the books, running your hands over them, sometimes squatting down on the floor to look carefully at the books kept on the bottom shelf, and then bringing over a step ladder or stool to climb up and see the books that have been kept high up? Finding the copies of books I was searching for, or bringing down a dusty copy of a forgotten book that no one had issued in many years and taking it away with me to read was a thrilling new experience. Till today I read all kinds of books.

From St Xavier's, I went to Madras Institute of Technology to study aeronautical engineering. My hunger for reading had only grown by now. But I was also still rather penniless since most of the little money I got was used to pay my bills. However, I discovered a tiny bookshop at Moore Market in Madras (now Chennai) whose owner was happy to lend me books for a small deposit. I started reading through his collection in earnest, quickly making my way through the classics, translations, collections of poetry and essays. I found works explaining concepts from different religions interesting and I studied the holy books and texts of Hinduism, Christianity, Buddhism, the works of Confucius. The seeds for this were perhaps laid by my father, who was a deeply religious man and knew the texts of Islam closely. By now my mind was getting ever more thirsty and I needed to know many answers.

Once I started working and got deeper into the world of science the questions about connections between the worldly and the spiritual was something that intrigued me. How are we all connected? Does science negate spirituality? How can we keep our beliefs while delving into matters that require theorems and proofs to establish their existence? I read the works of great scientists and philosophers who have delved into these matters. Questions of morality and codes to live one's life by were also playing on my mind and the works of thinkers like J. Krishnamurthi, Ralph Waldo Emerson, Sri Aurobindo helped me to understand not only myself but the rapidly unfolding world around me. These essays and books helped me analyse situations better and read my fellow workers and their motivations clearly.

One work that has been almost like a code for living for me is the *Thirukural*. It was written by saint-poet Thiruvaiyur over 2,000 years ago in the great age of Tamil Sangam literature and consists of couplets or kurals. Each of these contains a profound truth or moral code, expressed in a few words but enfolding within astonishing wisdom. There has been hardly any moment of conflict or despair in my life that the *Thirukural* has not helped to resolve.

The other literary form that has intrigued and captivated me from my school days is poetry. I can still recall a few poems that appeared in our literature textbooks. Later, I read the works of Shakespeare and Milton and Donne. Milton's *Paradise Lost* has been a particular favourite for decades and I have read and reread those lines over and over again. The works of Indian masters like Tagore and Bharatiar and Aurobindo too have deeply touched me with their visions for humankind and deep nationalistic strain. The immediate passion that a poem can capture is perhaps unparalleled in any other form. I myself have written a number of poems and each time I try to distil the essence of what I want to say into the lines, I think of the great poems I have loved and admired.

As I grew older, I started thinking more and more about this nation of ours and where we are all headed. What is the role of each citizen? What does the youth want? What are they entitled to? What are their responsibilities? What is the vision that we need to keep before us as we traverse the path towards a better and brighter future for each one of us? At this time in my life, I also became a writer myself. I published my first book successfully and before I knew it I had authored quite a number of titles. With each one not only did I get to understand the requirements of a writer better, I started thinking more deeply on issues of development and vision. My reading became more oriented towards this as I had to understand large amounts of data, look critically at reports and draw inferences that would help lay out a vision document, one we called Vision 2020. Along with these, reading the works of Gandhi, Lincoln, and the histories of nations kept me inspired to keep working on the mission of finding ways to make India a developed nation in the near future and within our lifetimes.

These days, I hear that people are reading less and less. Perhaps there are more distractions, more gadgets, our lives are too busy to find a quiet corner and savour a book. Yet, this is a habit that we need to keep alive in ourselves and inculcate in future generations. Reading is to the mind what a good meal is to the body. It sustains, it nourishes, it helps us think, it helps us grow. I have for years spoken about a few simple things we can do in our homes and around us to keep this habit alive. I hope some of you will agree with my suggestions and try to implement some of them.

- Build home libraries. Gather books in one and twos and slowly build up a collection. Keep this library as a gift for future generations, filling it with beautiful meaningful books.
- Read with your parents or friends. Sometimes reading with each other gives you the enthusiasm to keep on reading.
- Visit bookstores and libraries when you go to any new place. Sometimes you may find more information hidden away there than you expected.

A list of some of my favourite books

Light from Many Lamps

Man the Unknown

Thirukural

Code Name God

Everyday Greatness

The Holy Koran

Bhagavat Gita

Holy Bible

Gitanjali

Paradise Lost

The Prophet

Hills, Bus Stops
and Under the Quilt

Subhadra Sen Gupta

It was a late afternoon in June. I was sitting on the veranda of a tiny cottage up in the hills of Manali in Himachal Pradesh. I was reading a book and occasionally raising my head to look around me. As a city brat growing up in the narrow lanes of Old Delhi, this was a view I had never seen before.

I could look far to the horizon that was lined by green hills, as the endless expanse of the cerulean sky seemed to dip and merge with the edges of the emerald fields. At home in Daryaganj, all I could see from our veranda was about two square feet of muddy sky and my friend Ranju's father shaving on the terrace. Except for a tough old *bel* tree that thumped down giant balls of fruit into the courtyard, nature was sort of absent from our lives.

So for me, Manali was a revelation, and it was made even more special because I was also discovering an amazing writer.

Suddenly it fell oddly quiet as the sun vanished, the sky began to darken and a flock of birds flew away above my head in an excited flutter of wings. I could smell pine and eucalyptus and hear the leaves begin to move in a soft clatter due to the suddenly rising breeze. The clouds started to gather like dark moving smoke just below the peaks of the hills in the distance, and then they began to float down, drifting in through the trees and above the fields of growing wheat, moving lower and lower until they engulfed the cluster of cottages—and me. That was when I discovered that rain clouds have a faint sort of muggy smell, like drying raincoats.

And today, fifty-one years later, I remember the book I was reading that afternoon, happily enveloped in the clouds of Manali. It was *Jamaica Inn* by that fabulous storyteller, Daphne du Maurier. It was the first Maurier I'd read and I would soon zip through all her books— *Rebecca, My Cousin Rachel* and *Flight of the Falcon*. And over the years, every time I read *Jamaica Inn*, I would flashback to that cloudy afternoon. It was a great place to read a story of dark happenings in a mysterious inn full of sinister people.

Jamaica Inn and Manali sort of matched, but what made me read about the Duchess of Blandings sitting inside a deserted temple in Hampi? Now for all of you who are unaware of the lunatic pleasures of P.G. Wodehouse, the incomparable Duchess is, in fact, a pig; a very, very fat one. She is a duchess because she lives in Blandings Castle and is the pet of Lord Emsworth, who is, umm... well, not exactly bright in the brains department. In the book *Leave It to Psmith* there is also a character called Psmith (the P is silent by the way) and there is a weird scene with flowerpots that makes me laugh just thinking about it. If I tried to connect the dots for you, I'd end up writing a small book myself!

Only a Wodehouse fanatic will understand the pleasure of reading *Leave It to Psmith* leaning against a carved sixteenth-century pillar as tourists wander about all around, chattering away in Kannada. Giggling over an English lord singing to an immensely fat pig in a Hampi temple could be considered kind of inappropriate, but Psmith would have *totally* understood. He once went to meet someone at a fancy hotel wearing a huge chrysanthemum on his jacket lapel!

I love opening old books and trying to remember

the places where I had read them. In my world there are good places and bad places to read books. Among the best are the river ghats of Varanasi. I read *Malgudi Days* sitting there at dawn, listening to the slip-slop of the river water flowing over the stone steps while the kids in a nearby *paathshala* recited Sanskrit *shlokas*, their high young voices raised in song.

The most dangerous place to sneak in a storybook is in the back row of your class at school, where the shadow falling on the page tells you that you have been caught by the teacher and will now have to answer a question that you did not hear.

For me the best day of the year while in school was 15 May because the next day the summer vacation would begin and two heavenly months would stretch before me, full of books and more books. The only problem was this torture called holiday homework that was created by some sadist in the education department.

So every time I settled down with a Feluda mystery or a crazy tale being told by the hilarious Tenida or Ghanada, my Ma would yell, 'Are you doing your holiday homework?' Then, after a sinister pause, 'What *are* you reading?'

What was I reading? What do you think? Was I crazy that I would read the soggy *dohas* of Surdas in June?

So ways had to be found to hide the fact that I was not studying. One was this huge geography atlas that could hide a paperback inside it. So I would sit on a window seat at a strategic angle with the atlas held up before my face, storybook inside. Sitting on the window seat meant that no one could creep up behind me. Funnily, Ma never questioned my sudden passion for maps.

The other strategy was to vanish completely from sight. As you very well know, if adults can't see you, they won't yell at you, right? My cousin Bubla and I devised a unique top-secret reading space under my grandma's bed. It was one of those old-style high beds under which she had two giant black trunks. We pushed the trunks to the sides and created a space in the middle where we would crawl in and lie on our stomachs on the cool mosaic floor, peacefully reading while munching on chips, biscuits, extremely oily achar, aam papad and other sundry unhealthy stuff.

The under-the-bed view of the world was an interesting one of feet walking past—dusty (Khyaliram the cook), cracked soles with faded pink *alta* (my aunt) and clacking wooden *kharam* slippers (grandpa). We also used the space to hide our treasures from our older cousins who were a bunch of ruthless bullies. So our precious tennis ball, marbles, packets of chewing gum, photos of

13

cricketers and Coca Cola cap collection were all carefully stacked on top of the trunks. The only person who knew we were there was Grandma, who would be sitting above us. So occasionally she would bend down and peer at us and we would glimpse her upside-down face as she mumbled, 'Oh, there you are!'

Bubla was into conspiracy theories and space aliens, and insisted that we only use sign language while communicating under the bed. If I forgot and whispered he would act as if the Gestapo was about to march in and arrest us. From class five to eight, we zipped through Sherlock Holmes, Enid Blyton, Agatha Christie, Sukumar Ray, Sharadindu Bandyopadhyay, Sukhalata Rao and stacks of comics and Bengali children's magazines.

I would also check out any book that the adults forbade us from reading. So I tried Dostoyevsky's *Crime and Punishment* and promptly fell asleep, and even as a kid knew that Freud's *Interpretation of Dreams* was pure bunkum. It was under the bed that I discovered that for humour there was no one like Shibram Chakaravarty and Lila Majumdar.

For a while I carried Lila Majumdar everywhere. I read her at bus stops, during lunch breaks, on the upper berth of trains, in doctor's waiting rooms, park benches... You name a place and LM and I had been there. I insisted on large, unfashionable pockets in my winter jackets to hold her books. As I was also fat, my winter look of thick framed glasses, frizzy out-of-control hair and a woolly jacket with bulging pockets made me look like the 'Bear of Daryaganj', as one fashionista cousin kindly told me.

When I began writing I unashamedly copied Lila Majumdar's storytelling style. I am still amazed at how, as an adult, she could get inside the head of children and see the world through their eyes. She was, and remains even today, the Zen master of the laugh-out-loud ghost story.

I'm sure all of you have read books in some very odd spots. Under the quilt with a torch (done that), by candlelight (load-shedding), behind trees in the school playground (even squirrels do it). But have you ever read books in your grandma's puja room?

Now I should clarify about my grandmas. The one with the high bed and trunks was my maternal grandma, my Didima, and she was totally in the grandma mould— all soft and cuddly and cooked like a five-star chef. My puja-room grandma was Thakuma, my dad's mother. In a later age she would have been the CEO of a multinational company. She wore these crisp white cotton saris, chewed paan and did not like cooking. Instead, she ran all our lives and her sarcastic jokes used to make me collapse in giggles. Cuddly Thakuma was *not*.

We lived in a tiny house where Thakuma had created a space for a puja room behind two strategically placed cupboards. Here she sat shuffling her beads, ringing her bell and occasionally telling Lord Shiva and Ma Durga how they were messing up the world. She would also stop chanting her mantras to yell at the cook and supervise the maid who was dusting the room. Nothing escaped her eyes or ears.

No adult ventured near the puja room unless summoned by the Boss for a lecture, and so I knew that no one (that is Ma) would drag me out from there to do holiday homework. Once Thakuma was in full flow, telling Lord Vishnu what to do about the milk shortage, I would crawl in and settle down behind her for a happy hour of peaceful reading. When she was through, she would get up, slap me briskly on the head and say, 'Get me a paan, idiot!'

She never ordered me to leave her alone because, bless her autocratic soul, she understood that for me, books were like food. I couldn't live without them. Though once when I absently leaned against her back while reading she hit me with her bell. It made a fantastic clang!

I have never understood how people can sit for hours staring into space, like they do in trains and planes. My worst nightmare is being stranded somewhere with nothing to read.

It happened to me once at Jodhpur airport early one morning. On opening my bag I realized I had forgotten my book at the hotel and the suitcase with a spare supply of reading material had already been checked in. I looked around desperately but at six in the morning, all the shops were closed.

I peered into the locked books stall with forlorn hope and even wondered if I could get away with a quick smash-and-grab, but a policeman was giving me suspicious stares. So I sat down, checked my bag again and there under the headache pills, sweet wrappers and other sundry junk, I found this tiny booklet. It had been attached to a kurta I had bought recently and it gave instructions on how to wash handloom clothes.

With a sigh of relief I sat down and read it cover to cover. Twice.

So if you want to know anything about how to wash and dry handloom textiles (keep away from direct sunlight), whether you can use detergents (no), is using a washing machine a good idea (maybe) and want a list of colours that can run (indigo, magenta and maroon) you just have to ask me.

Reading washing instructions at an airport...beat that!

Books for at Least One Library

Sudha Murty

I come from a middle-class teacher's family. In my family, as with many other families of teachers, books and knowledge were considered to be more important than money.

In our village, I still remember the way people respected my grandfather. He was certainly not the richest man. He used to sit in front of our house, on a mat below a shady banyan tree. He always held a book in his hand. In the evening people would come to him for his advice. Even the richest man, when passing by, would greet him respectfully. I asked him once:

'Why should the teacher be respected?'

He smiled and told me a story. 'It seems, some friends

of Arjuna, the mighty warrior in [the] Mahabharata, asked him why he gave so much of respect to his teacher Dronacharya. Drona was old, not as rich as Arjuna, and never ruled any kingdom. But Arjuna would always sit at his feet respectfully. When asked why, it seems Arjuna replied, "In this life everything perishes over a period of time. Whether it be diamond, beauty, gold or even land. Only one thing withstands this destruction. It is knowledge. The more you give the more you get." A teacher gives knowledge to students and I consider him the richest person. That is the reason a teacher is respected; not for his riches but because he is the source of knowledge.'

As a child, the first expedition I ever made outside my home was to the village library building with my grandfather. The library was situated in a small two-storied structure. There was a shop on the ground floor and on the first floor was the library. A big banyan tree stood next to the building. There was a cement platform under it. In Kannada we call it *katte*. In the evening, all the elders of the village would sit here. My grandfather was one of them. I would accompany him and he would go and sit on the platform after dropping me at the first floor.

It was the first of the many libraries I was to enter.

There were cupboards with glass panes so that one could read the titles of the books easily. Newspapers and weeklies were piled up neatly. Tables and chairs were laid for people to sit and read. There was absolute silence. I started reading children's books there and used to be absorbed in them until my grandfather would call me to go home.

Years passed and I became a girl of twelve years. By that time, I had finished reading almost all the books in that little village library. At times I used to feel bored going to the library as there were not many new books. But still I accompanied my old grandfather to the banyan tree.

One such evening, we were coming back after our outing. I was feeling particularly bored with the library that day. It was dark and the streetlights were blinking. My grandfather could not see too well so I was leading him by his hand.

Suddenly he asked me, 'I will recite half a poem, will you complete it? This is a well-known poem.'

I said I would try. We often played this game and I had learnt many poems like this. He said, 'If I have wings...'

I immediately answered without blinking my eyes, 'I will go to the neighbouring village library and read many more books.'

My grandfather stopped in surprise. He said, 'Will you repeat it?'

I repeated, 'I will go to the neighbouring village library and read many more books.'

He laughed and said, 'What an unusual way to complete the poem! Do you know what the original poem is?'

'Yes, I know.

If I have wings
I will fly in the vast blue sky
I will see beautiful places
I will meet great people
I will search for hidden treasures.'

My grandfather kept quiet. When we reached home he sat down on a mat and called me. He was tired but looked very happy. He took my little hand into his and said, 'Do you know, there was a great man called Andrew Carnegie in USA. He was a billionaire who lived a century back. He willed all his wealth not to his children, but to build library buildings in as many villages as possible. I have not seen America, but it seems any library you see in any village was invariably built using Andrew Carnegie's money.

'I do not know how long I will live, but today I realized how much you love books from the way you completed the poem. Promise me, when you grow up, if you have more money than you need, you will buy books for at least one library.'

It was a cold winter night. I still remember the warmth of his large hand in mine. He was old, and his hands had become hard and wrinkled writing thousands of lines on the blackboard with chalk every day. We were not rich like Carnegie, but certainly my grandfather had the richness of experience and knowledge.

Later in my life, I became well off. I remembered my promise of buying books for a library. Today, through Infosys Foundation, we have given books to ten thousand such libraries.

I'd Rather Read

Jerry Pinto

Some like to garden and happily weed;
I'd rather read.
Some like to run till their feet bleed;
I'd rather read.
Some grind and fry and churn and knead;
I'd rather read.
Some like to study. (Indeed? Indeed!)
I'd rather read.
Some make baubles of seed and bead;
I'd rather read.
So now I've brought you up to speed.
Whatever others do, I'd rather read.
So don't you beg and don't you plead.

I won't play in the team you lead.
I know it's an eleventh man you need
But
    I'd rather read.

The Island Within

Anita Nair

I am not certain at what point in my life I actually decided that writing fiction was what my life was going to be about. But I know for a fact how I decided to become a traveller, and because travel had to be paid for, a travel writer.

All through the school year I made a promise to myself on how I was going to fashion my summer vacation—waking up to a bicycle ride into the dawn; fat warm mornings under the mango trees; the stillness of afternoon lying on the floor reading a book while the hand reached for a curl of *murukku*; games of badminton in the evening; long hours of the night, stargazing. Of a summer vacation when I did whatever I wanted simply because I felt like doing so and not because it was expected of me.

Inevitably after the first week of doing nothing but gorging myself on mangoes and *murukkus*, bicycling and badminton, and reading every book I owned many times over, borrowing the same books from the libraries and friends, a certain flatness would sink in.

I learnt the words of every popular song and sang along. I made a castle of injection bottles and a shopping bag of plastic wires. And yet the hours dragged. It was probably in those days, when the summer vacation seemed like a purgatory to go through before school reopened, that I first started reading whatever came my way instead of what everyone else was reading. And I waited for my father to make the announcement: The book tent is here. Do you want to go this Sunday?

For many of us growing up from the mid-1970s to the early '80s, the Soviet Union was more than just a country that covered a large chunk of Asia in the maps. It was India's closest ally at that point of time, and so the Soviet Union was also about the Russian circus, *dasvidanya* from Raj Kapoor's *Mera Naam Joker, Sputnik* magazine and the book tents.

As a small-town child, the book tents were the closest I had to a bookshop. A place where I could browse and, because the books were relatively so inexpensive, where I could buy a book for the cost of a comic. Over the years I acquired many titles from the Soviet book tents that still are part of my library. From Ukrainian fairy tales to Maxim Gorky's *Mother* to Fyodor Dostoyevsky's *The Brothers Karamazov* to a book of verse by Russian poets. I was a precocious sort, but I was only eight or nine, and so I read the verses and the Ukrainian fairy tales and ignored the rest. They seemed very difficult. What I really sought in every book tent was a book called *Kids and Cubs*.

My parents were a sociable lot and at least once a week they went visiting various friends. One of the friends' homes we went to every few months was a house I enjoyed visiting, unlike most others where I was afraid that I would blurt out something that would get me into trouble with my parents later. There were slightly older children in that house and there was a book I read each time I went there. My father's friend was a trade union leader and a steadfast communist. It was quite natural then that no bourgeois afflictions like literature would have a place in that home. But probably because it came from the Soviet book tent, and was about the various pets the narrator, a young girl, growing up in Alma Ata, a little town in the Kazakh region had, *Kids and Cubs* was permitted entry in that home.

Children don't remember authors. They remember stories. A child doesn't read a book because it is fashionable to do so. They read only because the story speaks to them. Children start a book with neither prejudice nor expectations. That makes them a true reader in every sense.

But much as I loved *Kids and Cubs*, it only intrigued me about people in other places. What sowed the seed of travel in me was another book.

In the summer of '74, a neighbour's young brother, Babu, came to stay in the flat above mine. He knew how to fashion aluminum crosses, build matchbox houses and tell stories. And he also had with him a second-hand book. It was *The Coral Island* by R.M. Ballantyne.

However, Babu's book was like entering a magical cavern. *The Coral Island* was enhanced by line drawings and colour plates by Leo Bates. I remember the first time I browsed through the book. I remember pausing at the first colour plate of an island chief with a cock under his arm, talking to the captain of the ship while a young boy looked on. It had me mesmerized. Babu let me borrow the book and eventually gave it to me as a goodbye gift, for he said he had never seen anyone as enchanted by a book as I was by *The Coral Island*.

Imagine this: an eight-year-old girl in pigtails and soda-bottle glasses holding a book so close to her nose that she sniffs at the old sweet smell of the pages even as her eyes race across the print. A spell is cast by words and pictures. Somewhere beyond the suburb she lived in, a little military township where they made armoured tanks, was a whole world waiting. A world of sharks and candle nuts, phosphorescence in caves and penguins, blow holes and strange customs.

I loved the sweep of the story, the adventures the three boys, Jack Martin, Peterkin Gay and Ralph Rover, get up to after they set sail in the *Arrow* and it is wrecked in a storm amidst the coral islands in the Pacific. But what made it that much more real and immediate for me were the illustrations and the colour plates. I had two particular favourites. One was of the boys coming across a sow and her many piglets sleeping beneath a yellow plum tree. And the other was of Peterkin brandishing a cudgel in the face of a penguin.

I had never seen a plum, red, yellow or purple, in my life. So I substituted it with a fruit I was familiar with. The sapodilla. In Chennai there were plenty of sapodillas and I knew the taste and aroma of the fruit. I hadn't seen a penguin either. And for the penguin I sought the curmudgeonly behaviour of a younger cousin. I created a world of wonder with what I knew and what I imagined it to be.

I was too young to question the veracity of the story I was reading and as an adult I resolutely stayed away from checking how authentic the adventures were, or even just how plausible. I was in love with an alternate world and wanted to keep that flame steadfast for as long as I could.

Old-fashioned colour plates have a certain magic. Almost sixty-three years after the copy I have with me was printed, the tonality and texture of the paintings are just as magnificent. The book is much thumbed. All through my childhood I read it every few months. Each time a certain drabness entered my being and the monotony of the everyday gnawed at my spirits, I went into *The Coral Island*. Lingering at the colour plates even as I read. Slipping into a secret world of my own.

Many years later I started travelling and one day, as I stood by a fjord in Norway, it occurred to me that for as long as I lived I would seek to do this—try and find the path to my childhood place of enchantment. That landscapes and customs may change but what I sought with every journey I made was that magical breathlessness I had found in *The Coral Island*.

Did Leo Bates ever think of what his colour plates may have done to change the life of a little girl from Avadi? Did he, by God, did he?

Do You Have Any Enid Blytons?

Roopa Pai

I wasn't particularly quiet as a child. But I wasn't what you would call garrulous either. There is no time to be garrulous when you have your nose in a book, which was my default position throughout childhood.

I coveted books. I lived them and breathed them and dreamed them. I bookmarked them and plastic-wrapped them and dog-eared them. I read them in the summer and winter and monsoon (but rather more of them in the summer, when the days seemed never-ending and school had receded to a distant memory). I read on the pot and in bed and while walking home from school (a dangerous habit that earned me a few hard whacks). And of course I read at the dining table, either while scarfing down food I didn't notice I was eating or while letting a favourite dish grow cold as the adventure raced towards its (completely predictable) climax.

I read comics and novels and books of verse and biographies and magazines and the English textbooks of friends who went to other schools and the newspaper and, when nothing else was available, the fine print on the fine paper in the medicine boxes—Neosporin, Burnol, Soframycin—that lay, poised and waiting, in a drawer in my mother's kitchen, part of her bristling arsenal against a world full of evil germs, all of whom had her children within their crosshairs.

But of all the different things I read, all the authors and genres—and all the different types of paper they were printed on—there was one writer whose voice filled my head and ruled my heart and lit up my childhood, at the end of which I still hadn't finished reading everything she had written.

And so you should not be surprised to discover that whenever we went to visit some distant relative or long-ago family friend that we kids hadn't met before—my parents were big on that kind of thing—and the kids had been shooed away after we had hello-aunty-hello-uncled everyone and they had oh-my-how-big-you've-growned us and pinched our cheeks, and after I had

33

gone breathlessly through the mandatory 'What's your name? Which class? Which school?' with everyone my height and a little taller and a little shorter, I would turn to the children of the house and ask the all-important, hold-your-breath-and-hope-like-heck question whose answer would determine the success or failure—for me at least—of that particular outing:

'Do you have any Enid Blytons?'

A 'Yes' would send warm fuzzy feelings gushing everywhere; these were *my* people. All that was left to do, once my eyes had demisted, was to raid their bookshelf, find a favourite old Blyton or a new one, curl up somewhere and begin reading immediately, my new 'friends' quite forgotten. In my defence, one never knew when the parents would decide to up sticks, so using whatever time there was at hand was essential. Of course, if the host kids' response to my question was a 'No' or a blank look, they were summarily consigned to the dustbin of my personal history and never spoken to again.

What was the peculiar magic that lay in those books—a mind-boggling 762 of them, which have sold over 600 million copies so far, been translated into over ninety languages and remain bestsellers with every new generation of children, even half a century after Blyton's death in 1968? It would take nothing short of a PhD thesis's worth of research and analysis to figure that one out.

After all, Enid Blyton did not write only one kind of story. Instead, her stories spanned the gamut of subjects and genres that appealed to a catholic and imaginative young reader like me—fantasy, fairy tale, adventure, verse, mystery, crime and detection, boarding-school stories, animal stories, Biblical stories and, erm, circus stories, a 'genre' that she created and populated all by herself. Sadly for Blyton, her output was prodigious enough to be unbelievable (what normal person writes 762 books?). She was accused, in her lifetime, of employing an army of ghost writers who wrote in her name, a charge she always stoutly denied, even dragging a school librarian to court for telling her students that.

After her death, and to this day, her critics have been scathing, levelling against her charges of racism (in her books the golliwog, a popular 'Black African' doll in England to this day, was often the 'bad' doll in the nursery); sexism (the female characters in her books, her critics say, mostly did girly things like cooking and cleaning, while the boys fixed broken things and rowed boats); elitism (everyone in her books was well-fed and well-clothed, lived in comfortable houses and had money to spend on ice cream); and, the unkindest cut of all, 'boringness' (educators, saying her writing did not 'challenge' readers, banned her books from school and public libraries in England).

Of course, as a child, I had no idea that my favourite author was guilty of such major crimes against humanity. All I knew was that when I had an Enid Blyton in my hand, the Indian summer vanished, making way for the watery sunshine of the English countryside. If I chanced to look up from my book, what I saw outside my window was not the coconut trees in the neighbour's garden but gorse and heather (never mind that I had no idea what they were then, and still don't) and the rolling hills of a cool emerald-green island, or the paraphernalia of a sunny seaside paradise (bathing suits, boats, pirates, smugglers, caves that filled when the tide came in, campfires on the beach and covert signals from lighthouses were very much part of the Blyton landscape) that existed only in my imagination.

Our family picnics always fell short of the promise that the word 'picnic' held, for were picnics not supposed to be about newly laid eggs; farm-fresh tomatoes; creamy milk; tins of tongue, ham and pineapple; potted meat sandwiches; just-picked apples; and a magnificent cherry cake that Joanna the cook had baked that very morning? Instead, my vegetarian South Indian household took along steel dabbas of lemon rice and curd rice; idli and chutney; and misshapen, falling-apart gulab jamuns that an aunt had laboured over the previous evening. They were all delicious in their own way, but they did not form a 'picnic' lunch. Plus, in our not-picnics, there were always adults around; in contrast, Blyton kids cycled, hiked, rowed, camped, stopped at little teashops for scones with clotted cream and home-made blackberry jam and, of course, picnicked, entirely by themselves.

I read Blyton through part of the 1970s and '80s, when the word 'sexism' was still largely unknown, at least in my little world. If her work was sexist, I did not notice it. In the Famous Five series, my favourite character, as of most of my friends, was the tomboy George (she hated being called Georgina), a single child who resisted gender stereotyping and owned Timothy the dog. In the Secret Seven series, I always rooted not for one of the Seven, but for Jack's sister Susie and her friend Binkie, who routinely disrupted the SS meetings chaired by the insufferably smug Peter. The cast of characters in Blyton's boarding-school stories were a reflection of the characters in my world; whether they were brave or loyal or clever or confident or sneaky or spoilt or scared or mean or fabulous at lacrosse—or not, they were all girls.

Was Blyton elitist? If she was, I could not have

cared less. I liked reading about kids doing things that I could never have dreamt of in my protected, coddled and circumscribed existence. I liked reading about exotic places and people who owned islands and ate unfamiliar food. It didn't make me feel deprived in the least; on the contrary, it showed me that the world was a big place, full of joyful possibilities. What's more, it allowed me to explore it all, if only through my imagination. I loved that kids in her books always got the better of crooked adults and re-established order in some little corner of the world. I loved that fairness, honesty, hard work, kindness and a strong sense of justice trumped meanness, slyness, selfishness and dishonesty every single time. I took heart from the fact that good kids did not have to be moralistic little prigs but could have plenty of childish, harmless fun, usually at the village policeman's expense.

Racism is a serious charge, but I did not identify it as such in Enid Blyton's stories. That doesn't mean it didn't exist, but most of the white Western world was racist when Blyton was writing, and she was only a product of her times. Sure, her characters were all white, but it never occurred to me to judge them on the colour of their skin; to me, they were just children, but children who were also imbued with a strong sense of fairness and justice. I can say without the slightest hint of irony that Blyton was as responsible for fashioning my moral compass as the moral science classes at school, where the nuns counted off their fingers, in stage whispers, all the dire things that awaited us should we slip; and my parents, who threatened me with worse if I strayed.

But the most unfair, most unwarranted and yes, silliest charge of all is that Blyton is boring, that her stories are 'predictable' and 'repetitive'. As a lifelong and diehard fan, I am not even going to dignify that charge with a rebuttal. Instead, I am going to shut my computer and walk to the library around the corner. I am going to open the door, breathe in a few lungfuls of heavenly library smell and, with a mounting sense of anticipation, walk up to the girl at the counter.

'Do you have any Enid Blytons?' I will ask.

And I will smile, for I know that the answer—as boring, predictable and repetitive as it has been for ninety-three years, since Blyton's first book was published—will be, 'Yes, ma'am, of course we do!'

Finding Feluda

Jash Sen

I don't talk about the joy of reading much. Most readers know it all too well and have talked about it until they are cross-eyed, and still leave non-readers wondering what they are talking about (I mean, it's just a book, ink on paper, right?). But if I had to talk about the joys of reading *detective* fiction, I would be telling you about some of my best memories from childhood. Now, that I don't mind doing at all.

First, there is a tingling feeling in you as you pick up the book, find your cosy spot and settle down with it, some biscuits and a bottle of water, for a few hours of undisturbed pleasure. Then there is the breath that you let out in a soft whoosh as you read the title and the first sentence—the 'here goes' breath. Over the next few hours, you will hold your breath, you will breathe shallow out of excitement, but you won't know it, for the story will build up tension and all you will remember is to munch on a biscuit every time it gets too tense. Then will come the point of no return and bedtime, usually at the same time; you will wait until the house is silent, forcing yourself to stay awake, then cautiously switch on the torch under your coverlet to read that all-important last chapter. Your breath will now come out in a much larger, louder sigh of satisfaction, just before you drift off to a surprisingly blissful sleep.

These are the golden rules of detective fiction reading.

Each one is also a golden memory that I have savoured in my solitary moments. Now that I know you are interested and so we must be friends, here they are:

1. **Age seven:** Late-night reading with a torch inside the mosquito net.

The Secret Room
by Enid Blyton

I read quite a few books under torchlight. I used to sleep in my own room since I was a child and 'lights out' was only a challenge meant to be overcome by quick thinking. The torch batteries would die in a matter of days, so it did mean my grandfather suspecting that he was being sold adulterated ones, but detective fiction fans have to be brave and not let these trifles come in their way.

Featuring the Five Find-Outers and their dog, Buster, this book taught me that orange juice could be used as invisible ink, which I tried out with limited success (I still had some blue ink left in my fountain pen). It also taught me how to get out of a locked room, which, sadly, I never did get the opportunity to try out. I especially remember this book because I finished it and immediately realized that I needed to go to the toilet, as I had drunk several gallons of water while reading. That was a noisy procedure in a hundred-year-old house with a creaky wooden door. At 1 a.m. it was very noisy indeed. I woke up the dog, the household and the staff, then the street dogs as well.

2. **Age Eight:** An unexpected summertime tragedy.

Kailash Chowdhuryr Pathor
(Kailash Chowdhury's Stone)
by Satyajit Ray

This was my first Feluda adventure. It was towards the end of the anthology of Feluda stories, but the illustration of the man with a big gemstone and curly moustache got me hooked as soon as I leafed through it for the first time. As I read about Kailash Chowdhury, his evil twin Kedar and the invaluable gemstone, I made a terrible mistake, never to be repeated—I licked an orange rocket ice lolly. Sure enough, tragedy struck when a sizeable chunk of the orange rocket fell on said illustration, thereby leading to a waste of both ice lolly and book. Which is why I mention only water in my golden rules, see?

3. **Age nine:** Summer afternoons on a broad window ledge while everyone had their siesta.

Shonar Kella (*The Golden Fortress*)
by Satyajit Ray

There is a special joy in reading detective or

ghost stories in an utterly silent house. It is as if the whole house is conspiring to create the right atmosphere for you. The ceiling fan swishes, the tap drips steadily, and old wooden doors and windows creak as they expand in the heat.

To me, *The Golden Fortress* will always be the definitive Feluda story. This was the book that made me fall in love with geometry and Rajasthan, a state I would live in for the next five years of my life. It was way ahead of anything I had read until then in the genre and talked about parapsychology, advanced geometry and reincarnation, in a breezy style that no child could find difficult. I read it on my favourite window ledge for a few successive afternoons during the summer holidays and it changed my world.

It made me want to be a writer.

4. **Age ten:** Reading all the Byomkesh Bakshi mysteries one Puja vacation when everyone thought I was doing my homework.

> *Saradindu Omnibus*, Volumes 1 and 2
> by Saradindu Bandopadhyay

This was ridiculously easy, as I recall. All it required was removing the books beforehand and stowing them in the study-table drawer, then telling the adults that the loudspeaker was unbearable and I would need to shut the door to concentrate, and voila! I did have to practise my grave face a bit, but I just pretended that I was Byomkesh investigating a drug peddler's murder in crime-ridden Chinatown. Byomkesh Bakshi was my introduction to adult detective fiction. *Romance was allowed.*

5. **Age eleven:** Staring at the midnight moon outside my bedroom window.

The Hound of the Baskervilles
by Sir Arthur Conan Doyle

Rajasthan had the quietest nights imaginable and the most stars I had ever seen in my life, for desert skies are crystal clear. There was no air cooler in my room and I would read late into the night until I was so sleepy that the heat didn't matter. One searing hot evening, I read *The Hound of the Baskervilles*. By the time I had finished, it was past midnight, but the horror of the story had not yet left me. I looked out of the window to find a reassuringly large silver moon and a carpet of stars. Why do detective stories, so full of violence, leave us with such a sense of calm afterwards?

6. **Age twelve:** Frantically calling my parents after the seventh murder.

And Then There Were None
by Agatha Christie

Small towns of my childhood were silent in the way nothing is silent any more. There were no televisions. On winter nights, by eight in the evening, everyone would be in bed and the chowkidar would be out, clanging the metal gates with his stick as he did his rounds. There would be no other sound until he came back. If you peered out, you would see hazy streetlights dimly blinking through the fog.

On one such cold, silent winter night, I sat at home and breathlessly read this book while my parents were out for a pre-Christmas dinner party. As I read about the ten people being murdered one by one, it got later and quieter. Finally, at about 10.30 and into the seventh murder, my nerves gave out. This is the only story I have read where I have called my parents and asked them to rush back home because I was terrified.

These are just a few of my reading memories. What are yours?

My Desert Island

Ruskin Bond

Games were compulsory in most boarding schools. They were supposed to turn you into real men, even if your IQ remained at zero.

This commitment to the values of the playing fields of Eton and Rugby meant that literature came very low on the list of the school's priorities. We had a decent enough library, consisting mainly of books that had been gifted to the school; but as reading them wasn't compulsory (as opposed to boxing and cricket), the library was an island seldom inhabited except by one shipwrecked and literary young man—yours truly.

My housemaster, Mr Brown, realizing that I was a bookish boy, had the wisdom to put me in charge of the library. This meant that I had access to the keys, and that I could visit that storeroom of books whenever I liked.

The Great Escape!

And so, whenever I could dodge cricket nets or PT (physical training), or swimming lessons, or extra classes of any kind, I would ship away to my desert island and there, surrounded by books in lieu of coconut palms, read or wrote or dawdled or dreamt, secure in the knowledge that no one was going to disturb me, since no one else was interested in reading books.

Today, teachers and parents and the world at large complain that the reading habit is dying out, that youngsters don't read, that no one wants books. Well, all I can say is that they never did! If reading is a minority pastime today it was even more so sixty years ago. And there was no television then, no Internet, no Facebook, no tweeting and twittering, no video games, no DVD players, none of the distractions that we blame today for the decline in the reading habit.

In truth, it hasn't declined. I keep meeting young people who read, and many who want to write. This was not the case when I was a boy. If I was asked what I wanted to do after school, and I said, 'I'm going to be a writer,' everyone would laugh. Writers were eccentric creatures who lived on the moon or in some never-never land; they weren't real. So I stopped saying I was going to be a writer and instead said I was going to be a detective. Somehow, that made better sense. After all, Dick Tracy was a comic-book hero. And there was a radio series featuring Bulldog Drummond, a precursor to James Bond.

In the library, I soon had many good friends—Dickens and Chekhov and Maupassant and Barrie and Somerset Maugham and Hugh Walpole and P.G. Wodehouse and many others, and even Bulldog Drummond, whose adventures were set forth by 'Sapper', whose real name was H.C. McNeile.

Pseudonyms were popular once. 'Saki' was H.H. Munro. 'O. Henry' was William Porter. 'Mark Twain' was Samuel Clemens. 'Ellery Queen' was two people.

My own favourite [author] was 'A Modern Sinbad', who wrote some wonderful sea stories—*Spin a Yarn Sailor* (1934), a battered copy still treasured by me, full of great storms and colourful ships' captains, and sailors singing shanties; but I have never been able to discover his real name, and his few books are hard to find. Perhaps one of my young computer-friendly readers can help!

Apart from Tagore, there were very few Indian authors writing in English in the 1940s. R.K. Narayan's first book was introduced to the world by Graham Greene, Mulk Raj Anand's by E.M. Forster; they were followed in the 1950s by Raja Rao, Attia Hosain, Khushwant Singh, Sudhin Ghose, G.V. Desani and Kamala Markandaya.

A few years ago, while I was sitting at my desk in Ivy Cottage (where I am sitting right now), a dapper little gentleman appeared in my doorway and introduced himself. He was none other than Mulk Raj Anand, aged ninety (he lived to be ninety-nine). He spent over an hour with me, talking about books, and I told him I'd read his novel *Coolie* while I was still at school in Simla— Simla being the setting for the novel. When he left, he thrust a ten-rupee note into little Siddharth's pocket. Siddharth, my great-grandson, was then only three or four and doesn't remember the occasion; but it was a nice gesture on the part of that Grand Old Man of Letters.

But I digress. I grow old and inclined to ramble. I should take T.S. Eliot's advice and wear the bottoms of my trousers rolled (and yes, they are beginning to look a little frayed and baggy). Is this what they call 'existential writing'? Or 'stream of consciousness'?

Back to my old school library. Yes, *my* library, since no one else seemed to bother with it. And from reading, it was only a short step to writing. A couple of spare exercise books were soon filled with my observations on school life—friends, foes, teachers, the headmaster's buxom wife, dormitory fights, the tuck shop and the mysterious disappearance of a senior prefect who was later found 'living in sin' with a fading film star (thirty years his senior) in a villa near Sanjauli. Well, that was his great escape from the tedium of boarding-school life.

It was not long before my magnum opus fell into the hands of my class teacher who passed it on to the headmaster, who sent for me and gave me a flogging. The exercise books were shredded and thrown into his wastepaper basket. End of my first literary venture.

But the seed had been sown, and I was not too upset. If the world outside could accommodate other writers, it could accommodate me too. My time would come.

In the meantime, there were books and authors to be discovered. A lifetime of reading lay ahead. Old books, new books, classics, thrillers, stories short and tall, travelogues, histories, biographies, comedies, comic strips, poems, memories, fantasies, fables…The adventure would end only when the lights went out for ever.

'Lights out!' called the master on duty, making his rounds of the dormitories.

Out went the lights.

And out came my little pocket torch, and whatever book I was immersed in, and with my head under the blanket I would read on for another twenty or thirty minutes, until sleep overcame me.

And in that sleep what dreams would come...dreams crowded with a wonderful cast of characters, all jumbled up, but each one distinct and alive, coming up to me and shaking me by the hand; Mr Pickwick, Sam Weller, Aunt Betsey Trotwood, Mr Dick, Tom Sawyer, Long John Silver, Lemuel Gulliver, the Mad Hatter, Alice, Mr Toad of Toad Hall, Hercule Poirot, Jeeves, Lord Emsworth, Kim, the Lama, Mowgli, Dick Tufpin, William Brown, Nero Wolfe, Ariel, Ali Baba, Snow White, Cinderella, Shakuntala, John Gilpin, Sherlock Holmes, Dr Watson, Peter and Wendy, Captain Hook, Richard Hannay, Allan Quatermain, Sexton Blake, Desperate Dan, old Uncle Tom Cobley and all.

The House With Many Treasures

Andaleeb Wajid

There were many reasons why I loved my grandmother's house in Vellore. It was an old crumbling house, huge and musty, and had a swing as big as a bed. It was the place where we went in summer, where we were relentlessly pampered by my grandmother, cousins running around the terrace, sweaty, hungry and sitting down to play a game of cards on sleepy warm afternoons. But more than all this, I loved that house because of the many treasures one could find there if one looked hard enough.

By treasures, I mean books. Dusty books without covers, some riddled with holes made by silverfish that wriggled away slowly when we opened them. Louis

54

L'Amour was one of my uncle's favourite authors, so there was always a chance that we would find his books stashed in some cupboard, under a beaded bag or a pile of newspapers. I was not such a fan of Westerns, so they were often dumped back from whichever corner I would discover them. Then there were the Mills and Boons my aunt read, but those were almost always borrowed from libraries and there was a sense of grown-up-ness about them, so I was a little wary of them.

Then there were the books without covers that became so much more mysterious to us. There was no Google then, so we couldn't do a search for the author name and try to figure out which book this could be. Often, reading a book without a cover was an adventure that we were a bit reluctant to get into. It would mean spending time over something that may not pay off at all because even though I could see the name of the book or author on the headers, it meant nothing without the cover. In fact, it could be a boring Western, for all I knew!

What my brother and I loved the most was discovering the comics that my aunt had collected over the years. I can remember many an afternoon spent poring over Mandrake the Magician and his feats with his strongman Lothar, or discovering the Phantom comics and reading them in the order they came out. The stories were fantastic, the locations were often unpronounceable (try pronouncing Xanadu!) but the inroads these made into our imagination were huge!

We were often transported to these magical worlds, each in our own bubble of contentment as we read and re-read these comics. Phantom, his pygmies and his bond with his horse Hero, or his scary wolf Devil who often ran beside him, fascinated me, as did his love story with Diana Palmer, the woman he eventually married. Every summer vacation they became my extended family.

These dusty yellowed comics were also the reason we got into fights, because there was often a comic that I wanted to read but it would be with my brother or my cousin, who would read it with excruciating slowness. Hurrying them was not easy, so I would often settle into a chair and stare at them relentlessly until they would give it up.

The swing I mentioned earlier? The one as big as a bed? It was the place where we liked to lie down and read. One of us would get down, push the swing a couple of times and clamber back on. I don't think any vacation, foreign or not, can bring about that sense of contentment we felt on that swing, where we would fall asleep, the comic books on our chests, waking up to a soft dusk and the clear sound of *azaan* ringing in the air.

My grandmother, a born storyteller, would sit with us some days and read out from an Urdu book of fairy tales that had a unique name—*Arabian Nights of the Birds*. For us, most of these moments were magical as we would listen to her tell us about the king of the white birds who had banished his queen to the far end of the forest because she had lied to him. There are many stories that unfold from that story, like a gift that keeps on giving.

When we were a little older, we were dismayed to see that the old swing had been removed from the Vellore house. Apparently, the roof was in danger of falling down and for all practical purposes, this was the best solution.

The house still had an air of containing many secrets that we had to uncover every summer vacation, but things changed as we grew older. My aunt got married and moved away and most of the thrill of visiting the house in summer dissipated, because my aunt was renowned for all the lovely baked treats she would prepare for us when we visited. Yet, it was still the place where I could lie down on a mat, stare at the criss-crossed ceiling, fan myself with a handheld fan during the awful power cuts and dream.

When my grandmother passed away, it seemed like the house had lost its core and couldn't function without her. My grandfather sold the house and moved to Bangalore to live with us.

What of all those books? Those treasures? Some of them were taken away by my uncle, the yellowed dusty Westerns and some Urdu novels as well, I think. Some, my mother brought back with her.

The Phantom comics somehow ended up with us. And they're there in my mother's house now, on my brother's bookshelf. I came across them as recently as a few days ago and picked one up, smiling as I settled down in a chair to read it. The smile never left my face as I let myself be transported back to those days of childhood, the yellowing paper of the comics bringing back memories of cousins sitting around in a circle, reading silently on a warm summer afternoon.

Reading habits may have changed over the years (or decades) since I was a child. But the truth remains that everyone loves a good story, and these are some of mine.

1. **The entire Phantom comics series**—However, the new versions that I have seen in the market are not as nice as the older ones. But then maybe I'm just too old, or too prejudiced. No harm in giving it a try!

2. **Five Children and It**—This delightful book by E. Nesbit is an all-time favourite. Five children discover a Psammead, a sand fairy, during their summer vacations

in the countryside. They realize that the sand fairy can grant them a wish every day. Every wish they ask for leads to hilarious outcomes as the wish gets undone at the end of the day. For instance, they once ask for wings, fly to the top of a church (I think) and fall asleep. When they wake up, their wings have gone! How are they to get down?

3. **The Sisterhood of the Traveling Pants**—This book by Ann Brashares is a charming account of four friends who use a pair of pants as a metaphor for their 'forever sisterhood'. They wear it in turns (an idea that grossed out my son who read the book as part of a reading challenge a couple of years ago) and the pants become more than an item of clothing. For each of the girls, it comes to represent something in their lives.

Growing Up With Libraries

Tanu Shree Singh

When you are barely three feet off the ground, everything towers over you. It is like living in a world of giants; you are constantly craning your neck to look at faces. So, on the first day of our vacation, when I tagged along with my mum to her college, I was standing on tiptoes to look at the face that smiled down from the counter and gestured to her left. I turned to see what she was pointing at. And there they were. Rows upon rows of bookcases. I looked at Mum's face for approval. Barely had she nodded that I ran to the first row. The top shelves seemed to look down at me and the books seemed ready to pounce. I remember feeling tinier than I was. As I walked on, a strange sensation tingled my nostrils and like any other curious eight-year-old child I drew a deep breath in to figure out what it was. The smell was old, musty, inky and spell-binding. I stood there for the next few seconds tasting the fragrance of books. It was only when Mum shook me that the spell broke somewhat.

'What happened?'

'Nothing.' I had a wide smile plastered on my face that came back every time I walked through those doors.

She let out a deep breath and said, 'I'll be back in an hour, okay? You can choose whatever you want and tell that lady over there to note the names down. Do not wander off anywhere, okay? If you want to sit and read, there is a desk at the end of the hall. Do not shout here. And do not cause too much commotion. If you want books from the higher shelves, ask for help. DO NOT CLIMB.'

I nodded like a bobblehead stuck on a car's dashboard on a bumpy road. I wanted her to go away to her class, so that I could inhale the books once more before exploring. This was the first time I had set my foot here. It was like a rite of passage to being a grown-up. And I did stand a tad bit taller than the 3 feet height allowed me to. Before that day, I'd always envy my brother when he'd come back with an armful of books from here. I did have my tiny pile of picture books that were a rage back then—the Russian ones translated into English. But they were just not enough. I craved for much more. And every year I got left behind because I was too young. Not anymore. I was finally old enough to touch the yellowing books in the quiet, serious shelves.

The first book that picked me was *Oliver Twist* by Charles Dickens. It was overwhelming to see so many big books and I stood there with hesitation written all over my face. A taller person looked at me, smiled, stood on tiptoes and pulled out a book from the topmost shelf. He dusted it and handed it over.

'Hello, big girl! Would you like to try this?' He looked at me over his glasses that seemed to be slipping off his nose.

I nodded and grabbed it. I forgot to say thanks, something that Mum had repeatedly reminded me of while walking to the library. My first 'big' book. It was too big at the time to warrant a small 'thank you'. I think I would have had the same feelings for a dictionary, had he given me that. This was also the book that introduced me to the habit of opening a book and holding it up to my nose to take in the years of fragrance. I think I did hear a couple of college students down the Economics aisle giggle. I quickly learnt to look around before sniffing books.

Back at home, I experienced tears while reading for the first time and I was alarmed. No book had done that so far. The ones that I had read before were all colourful and happy. Or, at most, had a certain Captain Haddock blurt out a trail of utterly funny abuses. But this one had tears, heartache and a dark sense of foreboding. I just knew that things would keep getting worse for Oliver but strangely those tears were very different from the ones that came when my teacher discovered that I had not finished homework, or when Mum found out that I had mixed a bottle of oil with a jar of flour. These tears did not make me want to run away or indignantly wipe them. I let them flow and turned page after page. Years later I re-read the book and was fairly amused at the memory of the three-feet-tall girl bawling her heart out, page after page.

The school library wasn't this magical. Probably because we were made to walk in with our forefinger stuck to our lips, in the silly hope that we'd be quiet. And once inside there used to be a tiny pile kept in the centre of a long table that all the kids pounced on. The shelves were strangely off limits. And if a certain girl tried to sneak up to them, she was caught and made to spend the entire period standing and admiring the cracks in the wall paint at the far corner of the hall. So Mum's library it was for the rest of school years.

Quite a few of my friends at school failed to understand why I always needed to be buried between the pages of a book and why I wasn't spending time adjusting my hairband for the 592nd time. I got called names and teased, just as my sons do now almost three decades later. But we do not mind. Being called a *kitabi keeda* is the most obvious thing. Of course I am a bookworm and so are my boys, and we are proud of the tag! If only those children knew what they were missing. If only they ventured into opening just one book and spent some time discovering the worlds tucked away between its pages. Alas! They did not. They still do not. They sadly do not know that the shelves hold secrets and promises—secrets of books not found in swanky online bookstores that display only the popular books to the sad exclusion of the good ones, and promises of adventures that leave you craving for more when the last page turns.

Sadly, the library I used to frequent lost its charm over the years. The librarian smiled a little less, a new one replaced her soon, and the books just crumbled. They were quietly replaced by textbooks. No one tried to find out why. Everyone was apparently too busy doing their job, completing syllabi and getting the work done, to bother. There were no public libraries, and my college library too was overwrought with journals, research papers and more academic gibberish than my tiny brain could handle. The world became a sad place. The only books I got were the ones I found behind the popular bookshelves at bookstores in Delhi. And Delhi trips were a rare treat, reserved for birthdays. So books were slow to trickle in. Faridabad had no libraries and bookstores, and it still doesn't. We are only raising serious textbook readers here, it seems.

Years later when my sons were chewing through books faster than I ever did, I came across a picture book that made me fall in love with the idea of towering shelves all over again—*The Fantastic Flying Books of Mr. Morris Lessmore* by W. E. Joyce. The book is an ode to books and librarians—my favourite people. Mr Lessmore's smile gets swept away in a storm, along with his library. He rediscovers the lost joy in tending to books in a surreal library which a flock of magical flying books lead him to after the storm. To see nursery rhymes share space with encyclopedias makes Mr Lessmore's heart swell with joy. And that somewhere set off an old idea that had kept knocking inside the little girl's head. She used to fantasize about being a librarian by day and a superhero by night. With more years added to her, the former seemed increasingly plausible with the latter ambition being handed down to her children.

One evening, I found my boys at the ripe ages of eight and six years furiously scribbling on a paper. A closer look revealed it to be a poster. It had a star-shaped banner announcing the opening of a library, a tiny postscript regarding the membership fees and some ill-shaped cartoons reading books. They had stolen my plausible idea. And they had it all 'sorted'. The posters were circulated but after two weeks of not a single inquiry, they shelved the idea.

I felt helpless. More so when I read Harry Potter and watched Hermione find solutions in the library books. We needed such places in real world—some place where we could find secret spells, where people like us could engage in a raging battle for their survival, where there was bravery and hope. People scoff at such places. After all, online stores offer the same books at fabulous discounts. So why go through the trouble of searching for a library, find it at the other end of the earth from where one lives, and then bear the glare of the librarian if you overshoot the issue period? What is the need for opening more libraries across the country, however small? Simply because it is in libraries that books truly come to life and sprout wings. They travel to places and find a wide variety of readers over the years. In the absence of libraries, bookworms like us continue to save up and buy books for our tiny shelves at home. Imagine if many such shelves came together at one place; imagine the variety of books that one would get to read!

So libraries have to survive. Not the manicured ones that keep books behind glass doors and let children choose only one book from a pre-assigned pile. But the ones that lure people in, somewhat like Mr Lemoncello's library[1], where readers get lost in the books they discover, where one book leads to others. You do not get the same joy in browsing online, clicking to add books to your cart and then ordering them with one click. The joy lies in opening the first page of the library book, counting the number of due dates stamped on it to figure out its popularity or being adventurous and walking back with the one that has had no stamp so far. The thrill of being the first reader is something else.

Anyone who says little children should not dream big and definitely not plan things beyond their scope should visit this tiny library tucked in a corner of a large building in my hometown. It was built by children. Cartons of books landed at our place because children from all over

---

[1] *Escape from Mr. Lemoncello's Library: A Puzzle Mystery* by Chris Grabenstein.

the country believed that libraries were crucial to being a child, and staying one. A bunch of kids showed up at my doorstep each day to do the boring task of sticking due-date slips and labelling the books. Each of them believed in the necessity of a library and knew that the size of the hands working towards that dream didn't matter. They worked with me every day to bring some more books closer to children who still hadn't discovered the joy of reading. As these books get ready to be shelved, I imagine them with a blank label, hidden in which is the name of the child that this book will someday belong to, the child who will set sail into the world of books using this book as the vessel. Each book has at least one child somewhere linked to it. All it has to do is wait patiently on the shelf for that child to arrive, discover that connection and carry that book in his heart. For every book comes predestined to meet its reader. It is just a matter of time. *Oliver Twist* was my book. It found me when I was lost between the towering shelves peering down at a tiny girl. Till then it stayed gathering dust at the top shelf of the library—a place where words meet eyes dreamy enough to hold them.

A library in every possible corner of every town will ensure that more books discover their readers. It could be a single shelf, full of books put together by tiny bookworms, or it could be rows upon rows of aging books waiting to be picked. It doesn't matter how big they are, as long as they are alive. And the only way to keep them alive is if readers of all ages, shapes and sizes come together and open the world of books to the ones still living on the dark side.

The Girl Who Ate Books

Nilanjana Roy

At the age of three, I was already a pest. This was mostly my mother's fault, though it is possible that I was born believing that the purpose of everyone who showed up in my life—the multitudes of beloved and loving uncles and aunts in particular—was to entertain me. In our rambunctious home in Delhi that overflowed with books and assorted guests, my sister and I were only persuaded to go to bed because my mother bribed us with bedtime stories.

Everyone's mothers and grandmothers tell the best bedtime stories; this is an article of faith. They didn't have my mother, though.

'Once upon a time, between the mooli patch and the

sugarcane fields that you see in the back garden, there lived a...'

My mother plucked stories off the cartoon figures on the cheap but colourful bedroom curtains, and made the tiny rows of sheep or the stars on our night suits come alive as she wove them into her tales.

She had the canon at her fingertips, and each night, she brought them all out, the wolves from the old dark German fairy tales, the bunyips and the goryos from around the world, the home-grown rakshasas and wizened crones who populated Bengali folk tales. Red Riding Hood tiptoed down the corridor on her way out to the forest. The Baba Yaga sat at the foot of my bed, and Pooh Bear dangled his paws over the headboard, leaving a jar of honey behind to provide me sustenance through my dreams. Brer Rabbit and the Tar Baby, who would both be politically incorrect today, visited at bedtime just as Tuntuni, the gossipy little bird from Bengal, hopped out of the window. But the best stories were the ones that my mother made up using just her imagination, where the lights would go off and we would be left with only her voice, transforming the prints on the curtains, the bed sheets and our everyday nightclothes into the stuff of magic.

Her storytelling created a small, determined and

persistent monster. I was notorious for toddling up to my father's seniors—stodgy ministers, ultra-respectable—and waylaying them with demands if my parents were unwary enough to let me into the room: 'Tell me a story.' If they didn't have a story, I would tell them my long-playing, revisionist version of Cinderella.

If this sounds cute, it was not meant to.

By the age of three, my relatives had learned to either flee or set me to errands in a vain attempt to ward off demands for more stories. The old stories had to be told just right, with the appropriate embellishments. It wasn't enough to hear about Arjuna stringing the bow at the swayamvar.

What did you make bowstrings out of, and did they have to be waxed?

How loudly did the bowstring twang?

If he broke the bowstring accidentally, did he have another at hand?

Did quivers have a separate space for bowstrings?

Why did the prince in Cinderella have to measure her feet, hadn't he been looking at her face?

Why was the coach that took Cinderella to the ball a pumpkin (such an unromantic vegetable)?

Why couldn't it have been a strawberry, to which I was partial, or a grapefruit?

The person at the receiving end of all of this was the kindest and gentlest soul in the house, the only uncle tolerant enough and patient enough to spend most of his waking hours being shadowed by a creature who came up to his knees and wanted story after story after story. (Even my grandmother had a three-story limit, after which she would retire to play Patience or to get some work done for the Women's Voluntary Service and the Time and Talents Club.)

The family version of the small pestering person in their midst is a funny story; my memories of the age of illiteracy are surprisingly dark. I must have been three when I realized that books contained stories, the way tins (if you were lucky) contained biscuits, and from the time that I made that connection, my mind was not at peace.

Those first thrills of discovery are fierce and unforgettable. So are the first discoveries of frustration, being denied something that you want so very badly—and that is readily available to everyone who towers over you and belongs to the remote world of adulthood.

I would stare at the ranks of leather-bound and cloth-bound books with a hunger so intense that the memory of it is as palpable as the memory of cold, or thirst, or grave injury. Here were books, within reach, many of them. They contained the stories I wanted so badly.

And when I opened the books and the magazines, one after another, black ants crawled across the page, silently, saying nothing to me, indifferent to my presence and my need.

My uncle took pity on me and at my grandmother's book-filled house in Kolkata, decided to teach me how to read. It is possible that he wanted to be able to retreat and draw plans of buildings without his niece attached to his leg, bawling because the story he was telling had ended and there would be no more stories, ever, but it was kind of him all the same.

I have no recollection at three of tracing the alphabets or learning the English letters, though from another time and place, I do remember learning both the Bengali and the Hindi alphabets. There must have been a stage when I went through the ABCs the same way as the *kaws* and *khaws*, but it has slipped the net of memory. By the time I turned four, my uncle's lessons must have taken hold somewhere in that hungry-for-stories mind of mine.

I remember the first words I read the way I remember nearly drowning in the sea off Goa once, the shock of the water rushing into my nostrils; or the way I remember reaching the top of a hill in Bhutan and stumbling breathless into the high monastery only to come face-to-face with a statue of the Buddha among the clouds and the jagged peaks. It is that sharp, and that electric.

The book was in hardboard, handsomely covered, a miscellany of poems and stories by writers so out of date that even their names are dusty today. The landscape on the front cover was uncompromisingly English, the meadows and polite rows of sheep and the cottage in the background with a stream running by it all completely unrelated to the cities I lived in and knew, Delhi and Kolkata. The pages were thick and creamy, the illustrations embossed in ink that did not smear across the opposite page even in the full heat of summer. And as I turned first one page and then the other, the black ants marched up and down, up and down, waving their antennae mockingly at me.

Then they slowed.

Then the words swam into focus and I could see them, and hear them as clearly as though someone had said the words in my mind.

Slowly, silently, now the moon
Walks the night in her tender shoon.

I said the line over and over to myself, some part of me knowing even then that Walter de la Mare's 'Silver' was terrible poetry, but what I was revelling in was not the words, or even the images behind them—the moon, peering out through a fringe of trees, in a dark night sky. It was the sense of power, of owning some words at last after having to beg them from adults for so long.

I turned the page and there were no ants. Only more words, and each word marched alongside another until I had read a complete sentence, and the sentence pulled me into the books and stories I had coveted and desired for so long. 'Shoon,' I said to myself, not knowing that it was merely the word for shoes, and a pretentious one at that. 'Shoon shoon shoon.' It was magic, being in that house filled with books, wondering how long it would take for me to read all the stories that all of them contained.

The celebrations in my family when they realized I was reading were heartfelt, most of all from my uncle.

When I was alone in the room, I said 'Shoon' again to myself, wanting to celebrate. Then I checked to see that no adults were watching, and hefted the book off the divan. I took it under the dining table, sat on the cool pink mosaic tiles, and hugged the book closer. If the words sounded that good, I thought, how would they taste?

Tentatively, I licked the page. I would discover later, through a process of trial and error, that Bengali books seldom tasted good, that paperbacks were dry and crumbly, and that exercise books were watery and disappointing. But the words 'shoon' and 'silver' and 'moon' had a tiny acrid bite to them. Like a practised thief, I turned to another page in the book and tasted the text there, just to see. Close up, the paper smelled a little like cookies, or like the waxed paper frill around loaves of plain cake. I let my teeth slide over the edges, stopping when Romen, the chef, came in and rummaged through the cutlery in the sideboard.

When he left, I bent my head to the book and with my teeth, tore off a corner of the page. It went down well, though it didn't taste of much except unsweetened porridge. Boldly, I tried a little more, pleased at the thought of eating what I had just read. Then I looked at the page more closely and panicked: instead of the tiny corner I thought I had torn off, there was a gap, a large tear, a perceptibly ragged edge. Silverfish darted through the older books like illegal sub-tenants, but even at that age, I knew I couldn't pass this off as a silverfish hole. The page was palpably gnawed.

From the bedroom, I heard my mother's voice. The adults would soon be up and about, the lid of the piano would be raised, and the house would rumble with laughter and chatter; and in the middle of all of this, I would be discovered for the miserable gnawer of books I now knew myself to be.

With trembling hands, I did what I had to do. Ripping out the page, I ate the telltale shreds inside the book, and then, piece by piece, I ate the entire page corner to corner. Then I quietly returned the book to the shelves, pushing it all the way to the back, and joined the household for tea, a little subdued. My conscience was troubling me, and so was my stomach, though this would hardly be the last time I would find the printed word difficult to digest.

Abridged and adapted from the essay 'The Girl Who Ate Books' published in *The Girl Who Ate Books: Adventures in Reading* (HarperCollins, 2016).

How I Started Reading

Satyajit Ray

I was born in 100, Gorpar Road in Calcutta, and lived there until I was five. Since then, I have lived in many houses, all in south Calcutta, but never in a house as remarkable as the one in which I was born.

It was not just a house, but a printing press as well. My grandfather, Upendra Kishore, had designed the house himself, but was able to live in it for just four years. He died five and a half years before I was born. High on the wall in front of our house, 'U RAY & SONS, PRINTERS AND BLOCK MAKERS', was written in large letters. To get to the press, one had to pass through the gate, go past chowkidar Hanuman Mishir's room and up a flight of steps. A huge door marked the entrance to the press.

The press was on the ground floor; the rooms for block-making and typesetting were directly above it, on the first floor. We lived in the rear of the house. A little lane to the left led to the entrance door of the residential portion of the house. The door opened to a flight of stairs. Those who had business in the press, turned left as they came up the stairs; and our friends and relatives turned right to go into the portion where we lived. The door on the left led to the block-making department, and the one on the right led to our drawing room.

[The children's magazine] *Sandesh* continued to be published for two years after my father's death. I can still remember it being printed in our press with its cover of three different colours. I usually visited the press in the afternoon. The first thing one saw on entering were the compositors who sat in rows, bent over their type-cases with different compartments, picking out letters and arranging them in rows to match the text. Their faces soon became familiar to me. All of them would look up and smile at me when I made an appearance. I used to walk past them and go to the back of the room. Even now, every time I smell turpentine oil, an image of the block-making department of U. Ray & Sons rises before my eyes. In the middle of the room stood the huge process camera. One man had learnt to handle it extremely well. It was Ramdaheen. He came from Bihar, and had originally started work as a mere bearer. My grandfather had taught him how to operate the camera. Ramdaheen was like a family member, so I thrust all my little demands upon him. I would pick up a piece of paper, draw funny squiggles on it and pass it to him. 'This must come out in *Sandesh*,' I would say. Ramdaheen would nod vigorously and reply, 'Yes, Khokababu, yes!' Then he'd place my drawing under the lens of the camera, pick me up in his arms and show me the upside-down image of it through the glazed glass behind the camera.

I cannot recall much about studies and lessons in Gorpar. There are some faint memories of an aunt called Bulu Pishi giving me lessons in English. The book she read out from was called *Step by Step*. I can even vaguely recall what the book looked like. My mother must have taught me too, but I don't remember taking lessons from her. What I do remember is her reading stories from an English book and retelling them in Bengali. Two of these were horror stories that I never forgot: [Arthur] Conan Doyle's 'Blue John Gap' and 'The Brazilian Cat'.

The business of U. Ray & Sons folded up soon after they stopped publishing the children's magazine, *Sandesh*. I was too young to wonder about the reasons. All I can remember is my mother telling me one day that we would have to leave the house in Gorpar.

We moved to Bhowanipur to live with my mother's family, away from Gorpar and north Calcutta. I was almost six at the time. I was unaware of the change in my circumstances, or that we had ceased to be wealthy and would have to live in a smaller house. I do not think children are ever bothered by such things. It is adults who decide who is to be pitied. It makes no difference to children.

I was not sad, but taken aback by certain things I found in my uncle's house in Bokulbagan, which was in Bhowanipur. The first among these was the floor in the house. It was embedded with pieces of china. I had never seen anything like it before. I used to stare at the pieces and think, 'My God, how many cups and saucers and plates were broken to make this floor?' Most of the pieces were white, only a few had the occasional flower, or a star or a wavy line. I could spend hours just looking at these pieces of china on the floor.

I had to spend much of my time alone, particularly in the afternoon. But I never got bored. There were ten volumes of *The Book of Knowledge*. I never grew tired of leafing through these. Then, later, my mother bought me four volumes of *The Romance of Famous Lives*. These were biographies of famous foreigners, packed with illustrations and pictures.

As a result of moving from north to south Calcutta we lost touch with many relatives on my father's side. The two people who continued to visit us frequently were Chhoto Kaka and Dhon Dadu. Dadu was translating Conan Doyle into Bengali at the time. He used to dress like a pukka sahib: a suit made by the well-known tailor Barkat Ali with a tie if he went out in the evening. He came to our house at least three times a week.

It was Dadu who told me all the stories from the Mahabharat. We used to read a chapter a day. I made him tell me one particular story at least four times. It was the story of Jayadrath being killed in battle by Arjun. I thought it was the most thrilling story of all. Absolutely fascinated, I heard how, one day, Arjun vowed to kill Jayadrath before sunset and eventually did, with a bit of help from Krishna. But that was not all. The chopped head of Jayadrath could not be allowed to touch the ground, for Jayadrath's father's curse would then work on Arjun and Arjun's own head would be blown off. In a rather clever move, Arjun struck the head with six more arrows before it could reach the ground, and made it fly a great distance to land in the lap of Jayadrath's father. Startled, his father stood up, the chopped head fell on the ground, and his father's head was immediately blown to pieces.

Dadu told me stories from the Mahabharat and Chhoto Kaka told me ghost stories.

When I was about ten years old, my mother and I went to attend Poush Mela, a festival held annually in Shantiniketan every December. I had bought a new autograph book, with a view to having its first page signed by [Rabindranath] Tagore.

I went to Uttarayan one morning. Tagore took my autograph book, but said, 'Leave it with me. You can collect it tomorrow.'

We returned the next day. He was sitting at his desk, which was piled high with letters, various pieces of paper, books and notebooks. He began looking for my little purple autograph book as soon as he saw me. It took him nearly three minutes to find it. Then he handed it to me, looked at my mother and said, 'He will understand the meaning of these words only when he's older.' What he had written was a short poem, which is known to most people today:

It took me many days, it took me many miles;
I spent a great fortune, I travelled far and wide,
To look at all the mountains,
And all the oceans, too.
Yet, I did not see, two steps away from home,

Lying on a single stalk of rice:
A single drop of dew.

One of my father's brothers, Subinay Ray, lived quite close to our house in Bokulbagan. He revived the *Sandesh* magazine, which had ceased to be published two years after my father's death in 1923. At the time, I was too young to read it. Now, after its revival, I came to know what it felt like to hold a freshly printed magazine and read its contents. Three different colours were used on the cover. It showed an elephant standing on two feet with a pot of the Bengali sweetmeat sandesh balanced on its trunk.

Among the contributors to the revived *Sandesh* was Rabindranath Tagore. His story called 'Shay' was serialized from the first issue. Lila Majumdar—the well-known writer—published her first story in *Sandesh*. The funny illustrations that accompanied her stories were her own. Another artist and illustrator of repute in Bengal, Shaila Chakravarty, also began his career by drawing for *Sandesh*.

There was another Bengali magazine for children at that time called *Ramdhonu*, which I liked very much. I remember how much I enjoyed meeting its editor, Manoranjan Bhattacharya, for I had read two of his stories—'Padmaraag' and 'Ghosh-Chowdhury's Clock'—and found them immensely enjoyable. They were detective stories, and the detective was a Japanese called Hukakashi.

I myself started writing at the age of forty. Stories, poems, novels, essays—I had never felt the need to write any of these earlier. I designed advertisements, drew book covers, drew pictures and made one film a year—that was my work. At this time, my friend, the poet Subhash Mukhopadhyay, said during an adda, how about reviving the magazine *Sandesh*. I agreed enthusiastically. In a few months the first issue of the new edition of *Sandesh* was published. I had not thought of anything new to write, yet as one of two editors I needed to do something, so I translated the poems of Edward Lear. I started writing to fulfil the demand that *Sandesh* created. Feluda's stories, Shonku's diary, all of these appeared first in *Sandesh*. Then I wrote poems, essays, etc. too. Since then, I have not stopped.

The Making of Bookasura

Arundhati Venkatesh

A children's books' writer must remember what it was like being a kid.

I have vivid memories of my growing-up years. Back then, we were given a library membership and a free hand. We didn't have adults attempting to foist books on us. They were too busy dealing with power cuts and faulty bore wells to bother about encouraging us to read. On the contrary, they nagged endlessly about posture or poor lighting and complained about our reading habits.

That's precisely why some of us read! But mostly we read because we found joy between the pages of a book. I remember snorting as I read page after page of William's antics[1] and cackling each time an exasperated Captain Haddock[2] used one of his colourful insults or uttered his famous phrase, 'Billions of blue blistering barnacles!' I drooled over the delicacies that Rusty's grandmother dished up[3] and fantasized about the Famous Five's picnic food[4].

How I longed to live on Kirrin Island and camp on Billycock Hill! Imagine my delight when, at age ten, we moved to a place straight out of an Enid Blyton mystery or a Ruskin Bond story. An old colonial bungalow that had a sprawling garden with chikoo, mango, pomegranate, guava and gooseberry trees, and a haunted house next door. We had snakes, hornbills, hoopoes and troops of langurs as visitors. The house boasted a view of a gushing river that would hurtle down a cliff a few hundred metres ahead. Like Don Quixote, I preferred fantasy over the real world. A lot of my time was spent staring into space, dreaming up stories and reliving those I'd read, with the sound of the river in the background.

On one such occasion, I was sitting by the window, reading about Rusty's exploits. I had just finished the

---

[1] From the Just William series by Richmal Crompton
[2] From the Tintin comics by Herge
[3] *The Adventures of Rusty: Collected Stories* by Ruskin Bond
[4] The Famous Five series by Enid Blyton

chapter featuring Grandfather's pet python when I looked out of the window. Imagine my surprise when I saw a snake draped over a branch of the guava tree, gazing back at me! I ran for help. When I got back the snake had disappeared and, like Aunt Emily in the book, I was told I was seeing things.

After that, it became a habit—the house developed the uncanny knack of conjuring props, participating in the story and bringing it to life. I was reading a ghost story, when I thought I heard rumbling noises. Yes, someone was moaning, and not just in my head! Rubbish, I was told, it's just the pipes sputtering, always happens in winter. The bungalow had been built by the British, and the plumbing was ancient. It was in a little hill town in the Western Ghats that got quite chilly. Still, it was eerie that there were spooky sounds every time I read a horror story.

Naturally, my brother was scared. (So was I, but I pretended to be brave.) One time he read a supernatural story and was too terrified to go to the toilet. But he had to. I promised I would stand right outside and keep saying his name. As long as he heard me, he was safe. If the chanting stopped, it meant he had crossed over into the spirit world. I repeated his name a few times and all was fine. But it was too good an opportunity to resist. I stopped saying his name after a while and began howling instead. A minute later my brother emerged, quaking with fear. When he realized it was me, not a banshee, he was more relieved than furious—at least he was still among humans, even if one of them was his pesky little sister!

When the grown-ups were away partying, we would have the house to ourselves. We would be up late reading, playing board games, having pillow fights and wrestling. Friends who were scared to stay home alone would come over; it was more exciting when we had company. The first part of the evening would be spent narrating a hair-raising story. 'A Face in the Dark'[1] was a favourite—it was just the right length and had the desired effect. There was also the gory tale of the previous inhabitant of our bungalow being beaten up by a mob of agitating workers—it was common knowledge and didn't need retelling. But we would graciously offer to show our friends the bloodstained walls behind the bathtub panels, an offer that was routinely turned down on the pretext that tummies were rumbling. After dinner, one of us would casually suggest playing hide-and-seek. The bungalow had lots of nooks and crannies. Each room had multiple doors, so two people could keep going around

---

[1]By Ruskin Bond

the house without ever meeting each other. In the sitting room was a spine-chilling close-range painting of a tiger that followed you with its gaze wherever you went. It was great fun to curl up in a corner making strange sounds, letting out a low growl each time the visiting friend passed by the tiger. The grand finale was to use the multiple exits to creep up on the unsuspecting guest and give her a good fright. We never had the same guests twice.

To reach school, we had to take the bridge across a gentle stream and walk up a hill. While the school subscribed to *Target* and *Junior Quest*, the musty neighbourhood library boasted a beautiful Russian magazine called *Misha*. The day a *Tinkle Digest*, *Gokulam* or *Reader's Digest* magazine arrived at home, a battle would break out as my brother and I vied for first reading rights. Whoever won giggled as Shikari Shambu and Doob Doob bumbled, while the other sulked and waited for a chance to seize the coveted magazine. Of course, this was anticipated and pre-empted by clinging to the precious object and carrying it everywhere—including the bathroom!

Books provided hours of entertainment, thrill and suspense. I held my breath when the Count of Monte Cristo or the Three Musketeers duelled. I rooted for

Matilda and cheered for Charlie[1]. I used my grey cells and learnt about poisons with Hercule Poirot and Miss Marple[2]. Sherlock Holmes helped me sharpen my deductive skills. Mr Bindle and Bertie Wooster[3] made me chuckle.

The fun didn't end after we had turned the last page. We would come up with our own silly songs, like Ernie's 'pomes' from Enid Blyton's The Five Find-Outers and Dog series. There were secret societies to be formed and mysteries to be solved, just like The Famous Five and The Secret Seven. A friend's garage became our hideout. We made badges and took pledges. Alas, we didn't have tongue sandwiches or scones! No lemonade or ginger beer either. We played badminton but called it lacrosse, and dreamt of tuckboxes.

Like little Jim in *Treasure Island*, we kept an eye out for the one-legged pirate, Long John Silver. We were always on the lookout for treasures and maps leading to them. We made our own bow and arrows with sticks and string and practised, for we were Robin Hood and his

---

[1] From *Matilda* and *Charlie and the Chocolate Factory* by Roald Dahl, respectively

[2] Detectives from popular murder mysteries written by Agatha Christie

[3] Mr Bindle from the Bindle series by Herbert Jenkins and Bertie Wooster from the Jeeves series by P.G. Wodehouse.

band of outlaws. We went hunting for wild boar—okay, I'll admit, we ran after squealing pigs—and imagined we had a feast, like Obelix and the Gauls[1].

Having a brother who was a war comics' fan meant occasional cries of, 'The Japs are here! And they're armed!' I'd scramble for cover as the broom-wielding house help entered the room.

We had our share of escapades, inspired by Tom Sawyer and Huckleberry Finn, and came home with grazed knees and bursting prides. Building a raft like Huck's and re-creating the Phantom's Skull Cave in the jungle—those were exciting times.

If anyone annoyed us, we would cry out The Queen of Hearts' oft-repeated line—'Off with her head!' We would eat a piece of cake and wait to see if we grew or shrank, like Alice[2]. We shared Swami's consternation at the question in his arithmetic book: How is one expected to calculate the price of mangoes without being told if they were ripe or not?[3]

We looked forward to train journeys because railway stations had bookshops and hawkers selling comics. Every

---

[1] From the Asterix comics
[2] From *Alice's Adventures in Wonderland* by Lewis Carroll
[3] From *Swami and Friends* by R.K. Narayan

time we travelled, we pestered our parents for comics. They usually obliged, and then had to put up with our improvised Superman costumes and Tarzan yells.

Our summers in hot, dusty India were full of adventure, just like Scout, Dill and Jem's[1], far away in Alabama.

I devoured books by the dozen as a kid, and I was quite the devil. Bookasura, the book-eating monster in one of my books, *Bookasura: The Adventures of Bala and the Book-eating Monster*, could well be me! Like Bookasura, I just couldn't get enough of books.

I now enjoy writing too. The fun I had growing up—climbing trees, escaping ferocious dogs, messing around with mud and worms, making up silly songs and nicknames, playing pranks and football games—all of it goes into my books. I get to relive those adventures every day.

I think I never really grew up, like Peter Pan. I still enjoy reading children's books more than anything else. Some recent favourites are:

Book Uncle and Me by Uma Krishnaswami—An utterly charming book about a young girl on a mission to save a pavement library.

Unprincess by Manjula Padmanabhan—Three bold

---

[1]From *To Kill a Mockingbird* by Harper Lee

stories about feisty 'unprincesses'. My favourite is the one about Urmila, whose looks are so revolting that flowers wilt and nurses faint on seeing her. I wish it had been written a few decades ago; I might have seen myself as a rather cool Agent of Mass Horrification instead of plain ugly!

Vanamala and the Cephalopod by Shalini Srinivasan— Vanamala puts up a notice in Thambi's shop advertising the sale of her sister, Pingu, aged eight. But Kanti Stores is no ordinary provision shop. A mysterious trough in the backroom gifts Thambi with pretty baubles on a regular basis. Whatever-it-is-in-the-trough takes Vanamala's notice seriously and Pingu goes missing. Guilt-ridden, Vanamala sets off in search of her sister. This leads to underwater escapades of the strangest kind. En route, all sorts of fantastical creatures make an appearance— the Tower Bird, the Lettuce Grower, the Boss and my favourite, Basavan the ~~bull~~ zebu.

Flat-Track Bullies by Balaji Venkataramanan—The annual vacation begins, and Ravi (the protagonist) has to fill up two pages of his handwriting notebook every day. The eleven-year-old does just that, while turning it into a secret diary. We get a peek into his thoughts as he goes from tennis, music, cricket and chess to IIT coaching classes. The author takes a dig at all the ridiculous things grown-ups propagate, from superstition to ruthless ambition. Refreshingly honest and outrageously funny.

Dear Mrs Naidu by Mathangi Subramanian—An inspirational story of twelve-year-old Sarojini, a student at a government school, who takes on the system. Told through the letters she writes to her namesake, the famous freedom fighter and poetess, the situations in the book introduce us to what the world may look like through the eyes of the less privileged.

The Queen of Ice by Devika Rangachari—A tale of intrigue. Devika Rangachari paints an unflinching portrait of the crippled queen Didda, ruler of tenth-century Kashmira.

Harsha Vardhana, by the same author, is equally riveting. The plot is based almost entirely on people who existed and events that actually took place. Not once did I get the feeling the author was trying to impart a history lesson, though; it is the story that takes centre-stage and unfolds most dramatically.

My World of Books

Deepa Agarwal

Once upon a time, there was a reader and she/ he lived happily ever after in the enchanted world of books.

I'm sure most people classified as 'bookworms' would heartily agree that this fairy tale is true. They are the lucky ones, blessed with a boon without asking for it. I always marvel at the fact that I am one of them.

How did I enter this charmed space? It was as natural as learning to walk, even though when I first began to leaf through the pages of a book that attracted me, our small town did not boast of a bookshop that sold fiction and other material for leisure reading.

Indeed, the launch of the first such store in my

home town was a very special event for us. How eagerly we awaited it! By chance, around the time when the bookstore opened its doors, my younger brothers and I received a generous cash gift from a visiting aunt. We did not stop to think twice about how to spend the money. Immediately, we raced all the way to the store, which was about three-and-a-half kilometres from our house. It did not take me much time to make a decision. Within minutes I had pounced on an abridged version of Leo Tolstoy's *War and Peace*. Sometime earlier I had seen my eldest sister turning the pages of a weighty volume with the same title and discussing it very seriously with my other sister, also several years elder to me. It made me very curious. What did this book contain that evoked so much conversation? When I saw it on the bookstore shelf, it felt as if it had been placed there especially for me. Years later I realized how significant this acquisition was—it was my introduction to the work of one of the greatest writers of all time. The abridged version led me to the complete novel, as well as to *Anna Karenina*, which remains my favourite novel.

But if we had not been a family of readers, would this vast panorama have opened up for me? How could I have discovered the social mores and idiosyncrasies of the aristocracy in nineteenth-century Russia, so far removed from our middle-class existence in a remote corner of India? What about the grand debacle of the Napoleonic invasion? And the interplay of relationships between all the memorable characters Tolstoy peopled his magnum opus with? It was just as William Styron has said: 'A great book should leave you with many experiences, and slightly exhausted at the end. You live several lives while reading.' I definitely led numerous lives while experiencing *War and Peace*, but perhaps Pierre's most of all. And at a very young age I was exposed to some masterly insights into human behaviour. Maybe the author's philosophy was a bit beyond my understanding then, but it was an enthralling introduction to world literature.

Time and time again I come across teachers lamenting how hard it is to motivate children to pick up a book. Over and over they request me to spell out the benefits of reading to reluctant kids. Sell a habit that I acquired as naturally as I learned to walk and speak? It dismays me that children receiving such an expensive education deprive themselves of a wonderful pathway to discovery. Worse, they don't even realize what they are missing out on. Because how can we consider a person who does not read regularly to be truly educated? Still, I try to set about it enthusiastically, and at the end of my forty-five minutes I fervently hope that I have managed to communicate my passion to at least some of them. But I cannot help thinking that I should be speaking to the parents. Those parents who never have books in the house because they think it's a waste of money, never read to their children because they believe it's a waste of time. And why? Because sadly, they themselves are strangers to the pleasures of reading. And for this reason, an engaging pastime has to be presented like a package—this is what you will gain by embracing this activity, this is what you will lose by bypassing it.

Often I share my own story with the children. How did my parents, who had very limited resources at their disposal, gift me this precious legacy? I'm not sure they went about it consciously. It was just something that was part of their whole philosophy of bringing up children. My connection with books was made when I was barely two, I think. Of course, now we all know that you can begin reading to children much earlier, even when they are still in the womb. But that is as far as my memory takes me. My mother would read to me from a thick book full of fairy tales and poems, a book with glossy pages and beautiful pictures. Later, I learned that these were the tales collected by the Grimms brothers, still a childhood staple around the world. At bedtime there was a different kind of storytelling—folk tales from our own country. Thus I had the best of both. The Grimms' book was part of a set of six volumes, and seamlessly the time arrived when I was able to read all of them by myself. The other volumes did not contain fiction but information about the natural world, the lives of famous personalities from around the globe and important events from history. I devoured them in the same manner that I devoured all the other books that came my way.

What did all this reading do for me? As I mentioned earlier, it transported me into realms quite distant from the confines of our simple small-town existence. Television was a long way off at that time, movies few and far between for us, but it did not matter. Because I was on a world tour, travelling through the universe as well and even back in time, magically, through the medium of books.

Books did not simply carry me away to new destinations, they also emphasized family togetherness. Some of my earliest and most pleasant memories of my father are associated with reading. A busy doctor, on a Sunday morning when he would relax with a cup of coffee, I would perch on his lap while he read out the Brer Rabbit tales and Phantom's adventures from the comic strips that appeared in *The Illustrated Weekly*, the most popular magazine at that time. How could I not grow up to associate reading with a feeling of warmth and affection?

It's not, however, always smooth sailing for book freaks. There are those ghastly situations when they run out of their essential lifeblood. Who doesn't know that awfully frustrating feeling when in the last stages of deprivation you reach out for anything that can be classified as the printed word—vague brochures, trashy magazines? At such times the dictionary presents a very decent and rewarding option that I can vouch for.

So, as a growing child, my biggest problem was how to feed my habit. My parents never thought twice about the expense when it came to ordering books but I would soon run through them, even those I invariably received as birthday gifts from family and friends. Thankfully there were other sources. An aunt who lived close by had an extensive collection and my brothers and I borrowed books like *Alice's Adventures in Wonderland*, *Gulliver's Travels*, *Little Women* and *What Katy Did* and a whole series of Walter Scott novels from her. When I was a little older, I also discovered W. Somerset Maugham in her library and went through almost his whole bibliography. My mother taught at the local government girls' school and no matter how unlikely it might sound today, given the condition of government schools, there were a decent variety of books, both in English and Hindi, in the library. The municipal library had a good stock as well, mostly of classics. Municipal library? I can see someone raising an eyebrow. Yes, such institutions did exist, though over time they have been effectively ruined.

When I went to boarding school at the age of seven, I gained access to all the books by popular authors of the time like Enid Blyton, Angela Brazil, Elinor Brent-Dyer (the Chalet School series), Richmal Crompton (the Just William series) and Frank Richards (the Billy Bunter series), along with the abridged versions of books by classic writers like Charles Dickens and R.L. Stevenson. During the holidays, however, it was back to scrounging around and I recall a neighbour with shelves full of Westerns—Max Brand, Zane Grey, etc. Was I too young for them? I don't know. My reading and comprehension skills were competent, so I could more or less understand what was going on. I sometimes think that these books were partly responsible for my leaning towards adventure fiction. Much of my writing falls in that category. Often, when I'm asked to recommend titles suitable for young children, I cringe to recall my very eclectic reading habits. I don't think it did me any harm in the long run, though I do recall that in the tenth standard our class teacher restricted our reading to the classics, in order to add elegance and polish to our writing style. Dear tyrannical Mrs Hollow! I have to acknowledge that her guidance made an enormous contribution to my English writing skills, considering that there was a counterforce at work— at home during the holidays, I sometimes turned to Hindi *jasoosi* (detective) novels. How did these books make their way into our house? They were often slipped in between the highly regarded literary works that arrived every month as part of a home library plan my mother had joined—the 'Gharelu Library Yojana' launched by an enterprising publisher. Yes, like I said, a driven reader will turn to almost anything. There was one genre, however, that I baulked at—the romances my friends were hung up on during our teenage years. They were cloyingly insipid, I felt.

My fixation with books remained pretty constant. There was a time when I couldn't go anywhere without a book, carrying one like my security blanket. I had discovered Russian classics apart from Tolstoy by then. My mother had ordered a set of them and I dove deep into Anton Chekhov, Nikolai Gogol and Fyodor Dostovesky, though I must admit I found *Crime and Punishment* rather disturbing. Well-thumbed copies of writers like Guy de Maupassant, Jane Austen and the Brontë sisters were also being passed around by friends and cousins.

We shared favourites like Jerome K. Jerome's *Three Men in a Boat* and Gerald Durrell's inimitable works. Alongside, I was zipping through random Agatha Christie and Erle Stanley Gardner titles, mostly picked up at railway bookstalls for the princely sum of ₹2.50. The action stories my brothers savoured came my way too— Alistair Maclean and others. I read Rabindranath Tagore, Premchand, Dharmvir Bharati and Devaki Nandan Khatri along with Alexander Dumas, Lin Yutang and later, Erich Maria Remarque. Also Shivani, a writer whose work had a sentimental resonance because she hailed from the same town as us and her stories had such a familiar landscape—both exterior and interior. And many other writers as well, too many to list here.

It was my love of books that prompted me to take up English literature in my university days, and thus become acquainted with so many literary masterpieces. Most important of all, it eventually inspired me to try writing my own.

Sadly, there are some benighted souls who insist that books are boring. To counter that I can well say that, early in my college days, our gang of friends discovered that we could battle the boredom of hostel life and entertain ourselves very effectively by reading P.G. Wodehouse aloud. As everyone knows, a joke is at its funniest in good company. It was one of my most memorable experiences of sharing books, and I relive it again when I read out their favourite books to my grandchildren and we laugh and exclaim together.

Yes, I can go on and on about what books have done for me. But I'd like to mention that a point came in my life when I felt impelled to entice others into this charmed world. All those students who earnestly proclaimed that they only read books to gain knowledge were responsible for this decision. How it depressed me that so many children were completely unaware that books could also be fun! The thought drove me to begin a book club. It ran for almost ten years at the India Habitat Centre in New Delhi and we had a wonderful time connecting in many different ways with new books and their authors. While some of our regulars have indeed grown up to be achievers in different fields, what I look back to with great satisfaction is how enthusiastically children awaited our monthly sessions. And why? Because they had made the magical discovery that all the quotations regularly plastered over their school walls during Book Week were from these books. That books are really your best friends, that they actually ignite your imagination, that you live several lives while reading—that there is no end to the gamut of experience a book can bring to you.

I affirm this because I have experienced it, and much more personally. And here I would like to end with a quote from one of my favourite authors, Neil Gaiman: 'A book is a dream that you hold in your hand.' To add to that, I believe a book is a gift box of all the possibilities you can conjure up to transform your mundane world. So read on!

About the Authors

Dr Avul Pakir Jainulabdeen Abdul Kalam (15 October 1931–27 July 2015) was one of the most distinguished scientists of India and received honorary doctorates from forty-five universities and institutions in India and abroad. He was awarded the Padma Bhushan (1981), the Padma Vibhushan (1990) and India's highest civilian award, the Bharat Ratna (1997). He also received the King Charles II medal (2007), the Woodrow Wilson Award (2008), the Hoover Award (2008) and The International Von Karman Wings Award (2009) among other international accolades. Dr Kalam became the eleventh President of India on 25 July 2002.

Subhadra Sen Gupta has written over thirty books for

children including mysteries, adventures, ghost stories, comic books and books on history. To her surprise, the Sahitya Akademi thought she is doing a good job and gave her the Bal Sahitya Puraskar in 2014. Right now she is waiting for a time machine so that she can travel to the past and join Emperor Akbar for lunch. She loves to travel, flirt with cats and chat with autorickshaw drivers. If you want to discuss anything under the sun with her, email her at subhadrasg@gmail.com.

Sudha Murty did her MTech in computer science and is currently the chairperson of the Infosys Foundation. She has written books in both English and Kannada on different genres. Her books have been translated into several languages. She received the R.K. Narayan Award for Literature and the Padma Shri in 2006.

Jerry Pinto has published fourteen works of non-fiction and poetry, as well as worked as a journalist in his native city of Mumbai. He writes poetry, prose and children's fiction in English. Some of his works include *Helen: The Life and Times of an H-Bomb, Surviving Women* and *Asylum and Other Poems. Em and The Big Hoom*, his first novel, won many accolades. He is the winner of the Windham-Campbell prize, 2016, for fiction.

Anita Nair is the author of five books for children, a collection of essays, *Good Night and God Bless,* and a book of poetry, *Malabar Mind.* Her novels include *The Better Man, Ladies Coupé, Mistress, Lessons in Forgetting, Cut like Wound* and *Idris.* Her new novel, *Alphabet Soup for Lovers,* has just been published. Her books have been translated into over thirty languages around the world.

Roopa Pai is a computer engineer who always knew she was going to write for children. She is the author of over twenty books, including the 2015 bestseller, *The Gita for Children,* and *Taranauts,* India's first fantasy-adventure series for children. She holds Enid Blyton wholly responsible for her acute and incurable Anglophilia.

Jash Sen is the author of *The Wordkeepers* and its sequel, *Skyserpents.* She is also a very big detective fiction fan. You can get her books from Amazon or Flipkart or on the Juggernaut app or read her articles at Scroll.in.

Ruskin Bond has been writing for over sixty years, and now has over 120 titles in print—novels, collection of short stories, poetry, essays, anthologies and books for children. His first novel, *The Room on the Roof,* received the prestigious John Llewellyn Rhys Award in 1957. He has also received the Padma Shri (1999), the Padma Bhushan (2014) and two awards from Sahitya Akademi. In 2012, the Delhi government gave him its Lifetime Achievement Award.

Andaleeb Wajid is the author of nine published novels— *Kite Strings, Blinkers Off, My Brother's Wedding, More than Just Biryani, The Tamanna Trilogy* and *When She Went Away*. Her Young Adult novel, *Asmara's Summer*, was published by Penguin in April 2016. She has another novel to be published in November 2016 with Hachette. Andaleeb enjoys writing for young adults but mostly enjoys writing about food, relationships and sometimes even weddings.

Dr Tanu Shree Singh is a lecturer of Psychology. When she is not teaching, she is found cataloguing the books at the Reading Raccoons Library, the first crowd-sourced, non-profit library in Faridabad, Haryana. She is also a member of the Indian chapter of the Society of Children's Book Writers and Illustrators (SCBWI) and has been writing for various online magazines and forums. Her first love remains getting hold of children and finding their match on the shelves in the library.

Nilanjana Roy is an Indian author and journalist. She is also a literary critic. She has authored books like *The Wildings, The Hundred Names of Darkness* and *A Matter of Taste: The Penguin Book of Indian Writing on Food*.

Satyajit Ray was an Indian filmmaker, screenwriter and short-story writer. Noted as one of the finest auteurs in world cinema, he is best remembered for his feature films, including *Pather Panchali, Aparajito, Apur Sansar, Devi* and *Charulata*. He was conferred several awards for his work, including an Academy Award and the Bharat Ratna. His literary works include his Feluda stories, for which he is best remembered in literary circles.

Arundhati Venkatesh went to school in five towns and worked in four continents. Everywhere, she joined libraries, read and made up stories. She went on to author four chapter books: *Petu Pumpkin Tiffin Thief, Petu Pumpkin Tooth Troubles, Bookasura—The Adventures of Bala and the Book-eating Monster* and *Koobandhee—The Adventures of Bala and the Book-barfing Monster*, as well as a picture book, *Junior Kumbhakarna*. She is currently based out of Bangalore. You can find out more about her at arundhativenkatesh.wordpress.com and email her at author.arundhati@gmail.com.

Author, poet and translator, **Deepa Agarwal** writes for both children and adults and has over fifty books published. A frequent contributor to magazines and journals in India and abroad, she has edited and compiled several anthologies. She has received the NCERT National Award for Children's Literature in 1993 for her picture book *Ashok's New Friends*, while her historical fiction *Caravan to Tibet* was on the IBBY (International Board on Books for Young People) Honour List 2008. Her work has been translated into several Indian and foreign languages. Deepa is active in reading promotion and is a resource person for Scholastic India, National Book Trust India and Ratna Sagar Publishers, conducting creative writing workshops and storytelling sessions.

Copyright Acknowledgements

Grateful acknowledgement is made to the following for permission to reprint copyright material:

Penguin Books India for extracts from *Childhood Days: A Memoir* by Satyajit Ray.

HarperCollins *Publishers* India Limited, for 'The Girl Who Ate Books' by Nilanjana Roy. Reproduced by arrangement with HarperCollins *Publishers* India Limited. Unauthorized copying is strictly prohibited.

Infosys Foundation and Sudha Murty for 'Books for At Least One Library' from *How I Taught My Grandmother to Read and Other Stories*.

'The Desert Island' by Ruskin Bond was previously published in *The Whistling Schoolboy and Other Stories of School Life*.

'The Wonderful World of Books' by A.P.J. Abdul Kalam was previously published in *My Journey*.